Model Contract Clauses

Phillip B. Wilson
Labor Relations Institute, Inc.
Broken Arrow, Oklahoma

ISBN: 978-0-9815085-1-1

Table of Contents
Model Collective Bargaining Clauses

This page intentionally left blank

Model Collective Bargaining Clauses

What is this book?

This is both a reference guide and a workbook. It can be effectively used to learn some of the finer points of collective bargaining strategy, particularly regarding effective drafting. It can also be used "on the fly" during negotiations to help refine proposals and counterproposals. The core design principle of this text is **practicality**. You will use it in one or more of the following ways:

A reference to actual contract language.

Employers or unions in contract negotiations can use the sample clauses in this book as models for their own proposals. An employer, for example, responding to a proposal on seniority provisions may not be aware of the many different ways that companies and unions have agreed to handle these problems in the past. The clauses in this text are taken from actual contracts. They provide examples of how companies and unions have resolved the myriad issues that often come up in collective bargaining. Experienced negotiators might get some ideas of ways to tweak language in their agreements. Beginning negotiators faced with a proposal for a clause they have never heard of before (what the heck is a "zipper" and do I need one?), will find at least a couple of examples here, along with commentary, to help them understand the basic principles behind most clauses that come up regularly.

A drafting guide for language. Most negotiators do

not receive training on drafting contract language (even lawyers – I learned most of what I know about drafting through trial and error). One of the best ways to learn how to draft good proposals (other than getting beat over the head with a bad clause you drafted during some later arbitration case!) is to read other artfully (and inartfully) drafted clauses. In some cases you will just copy clauses directly out of this book for your proposals. However, most of the time you will need to change the language to cover your specific situation. There are hundreds of clauses in this guide that can be used to draft your proposals. From narrowly tailored to broad and expansive, there are many examples included here. In addition, there is an introductory section for each set of sample clauses that highlights certain "key principles" for you to consider when drafting clauses in that particular area. Finally, even if you are drafting something completely unrelated, you can still get ideas about style and wording from the samples included here.

It provides options to help companies and unions reach agreements. Virtually all collective bargaining situations can be resolved if the parties wish to resolve them. One way to help resolve bargaining impasses is to provide options. If there are only two proposals on the table the chances are pretty good that the parties will each dig in to protect their own proposal. The best way out of this trap (I call it breaking out of a silo) is to get several other options on the table. Even if these are just used as examples (which many times can be better than actually calling it a "proposal"), the parties may be able to identify common ground. This can help to smooth negotiations and reach better settlements.

HOW TO USE THE BOOK
The book is laid out as an easy-to-use reference manual. The index lists all the subject areas covered in the book and each tab covers a separate collective bargaining issue. There are five sections to each tab:

- ❑ A quick introduction to the subject area covered in the sample clauses.
- ❑ A brief "drafting guide" that highlights the key points to consider when drafting your particular contract clause.
- ❑ A "plain English" summary of the sample clauses that follow (unfortunately most clauses are written by lawyers who have their "plain English" skills wrung out of them during law school).
- ❑ The actual model clauses.
- ❑ A ruled page for taking notes and for drafting of your own contract proposals.

That's it. Most sections have between three and five sample clauses (the most common subjects have a few more, the least common might have only one). The clauses have been selected for being representative examples of clauses you might expect to find in most labor agreements.

I have tried to include both pro-management language and pro-union language, to give readers a flavor for both types of clauses. I also include some solid "compromise" articles (really all articles are a compromise, but these are the ones that seem to balance the interests of management and unions). The reason for this breakdown should be obvious. The idea is to expose the reader to as many different types of solutions to these bargaining issues as possible.

During a collective bargaining session, particularly for a first contract, it would not be uncommon for management to begin by proposing something very pro-management and for the union to propose something very pro-union. In most negotiations the parties ultimately agree to something along the lines of one of the "compromise" clauses. However, depending on the unique circumstances of each negotiation, especially the bargaining strength of the parties, one of the "tough" sample clauses (for either management or the union) might be the one finally accepted in the contract.

You will notice that the language in each of the various clauses, most of the time, is very similar. Some clauses may almost look identical. As I introduce each set of clauses I make notes about some of the minor or sometimes very significant differences between the various clauses to give you some sense as to why a company or union would choose one clause over another.

<u>Also, I caution readers that some of these clauses are drafted poorly</u>. I do not go into all of the potential disputes that could arise under the various clauses (let's face it, under some unique set of circumstances every clause ever drafted can have a problem). However, I will occasionally highlight clauses where I believe the language could lead to disputes and give some suggestions about ways to "tighten up" the language.

As with any collective bargaining negotiation, the usefulness of the language and the problems that the union and the company may have in administering that language will depend on a number of factors. These include: the relationship between the parties, the specifics of each case that arises, economic conditions in which the employer or employees are competing and often political considerations within the company and the union. These clauses show how two parties, at a particular moment in time, decided to handle their individual situation. I make no warranty about the usefulness or wisdom of using any of these clauses in your particular circumstances. That is up to you, your legal counsel and your union. This book is not intended to give legal advice and if you have any question about the usefulness or legality of any of these model clauses in your jurisdiction you should contact an experienced labor attorney in your area.

A REQUEST FOR READERS

As a final note, I have a request. This book, like the collective bargaining agreements it summarizes, is intended to be a "living document." I expect that it will grow both in size and in complexity over the years. But I can only do that with your help.

If you come up with collective bargaining language that you believe is unique or an interesting way to respond to an issue area included in this book, please forward that clause (or clauses) to me for consideration in future volumes. If there is an issue area that is not covered that you think should be, I also encourage you to let me know about that. As a part of this project I am creating a database of contract provisions over the Internet. They can be found at my website www.lrims.com. I encourage readers to submit contract clauses to that database so that it can be a resource to other organizations around the country.

Introductory Clauses

Almost all contracts contain some sort of introduction that names the parties and the date on which the agreement is entered. Most contracts include only these items in their introductory clause. Some contracts also use their introductory clause as a "catch-all" provision. There are two examples that follow. However, the reader should be aware that there really is no "typical" introductory clause; practically anything that doesn't fit elsewhere in the contract could be included in one of these clauses. Some companies include things like the way the gender language is treated, general paragraphs regarding working together, discrimination issues and the like.

Clause Summaries and Drafting Notes

The first example of an introductory clause contains common "mutual agreement" language. It also uses "joint and several" language, binding both the union local as well as the international union. This clause also includes a paragraph containing general statements regarding the commitment of the parties to work together in the enforcement of the agreement. It also states that the parties are committed to "uninterrupted" performance of the agreement – perhaps a reference to a no-strike or no-lockout commitment. The usefulness of such language in arbitrations is dubious because it is not clear. How can an arbitrator evaluate whether the clause is violated? However, many times companies and unions will use similar language as a symbol of good faith.

The second version also begins with "mutual agreement" language. It then includes language regarding discrimination. This clause is more expansive than the federal and most state statutes, including prohibitions on sexual orientation, marital status and political affiliation. This clause, unlike the first example, probably does confer rights to members that will be enforced by an arbitrator. The difference here is that the clause is clear about what is prohibited. Companies and unions often include this type of language in a separate clause.

INTRODUCTORY CLAUSE (version 1)

THIS AGREEMENT is made and entered into this _____ day of _____, 200__, by and between [COMPANY NAME], ("Company" hereinafter), and, jointly and severally, [UNION LOCAL], [UNION INTERNATIONAL], ("Union" hereinafter).

It is the intent and purpose of this Agreement to promote a sound and mutually beneficial relationship between the Employer and the Union. The Employer and the Union are committed to the uninterrupted effective performance of the functions of the Employer. The Union will strive to maintain these functions through the performance of the regularly assigned and related duties of the classifications covered by this Agreement.

INTRODUCTORY CLAUSE (version 2)

THIS AGREEMENT, made and entered into this ____ day of ____ , 200__, by and between [COMPANY NAME], hereinafter called the "Employer," and the

[UNION NAME], for and on behalf of the local unions signatory hereto, hereinafter collectively called "Unions."

The provisions of the Agreement shall be applied equally to all employees in the bargaining unit without discrimination as to race; color; sex; national origin; religion; age; sexual orientation; marital, disability or veteran status; or political affiliation. The Unions shall share equally with the Employer the responsibility for applying this provision of the Agreement.

Recognition

Recognition clauses are very important in collective bargaining agreements. There are two competing interests at stake in these clauses. Companies typically want to have very specific language limiting the size of the bargaining unit in their recognition clause. Unions, on the other hand, want broader recognition language. Broader language gives the union the possibility to expand the unit in the future, claiming authority over newly created job positions or new company locations.

Unions are interested in expansive recognition clauses because they can increase their total membership and ultimately their revenue stream. Companies want narrow clauses (in some cases attempting to reduce the unit originally certified—which is lawful, although rarely agreed to by unions).

These clauses typically contain a compromise on one or more of the following basic issues:
- The job classifications covered, and sometimes the job classifications excluded from the agreement
- The company location (or locations) covered by the agreement
- The NLRB decision which certified the collective bargaining relationship
- Whether the unit can be expanded by the terms of the contract

The samples that follow include examples of both narrow and broad recognition clauses.

Clause Summaries and Drafting Notes

The first version is a relatively narrow, pro-management clause. It contains very narrow language referencing a specific decision by the National Labor Relations Board. It also specifically outlines the classifications covered (and excluded) from the contract. A company could utilize a clause like this in an arbitration case to limit the size of the bargaining unit—it could also expand classifications outside those listed in the agreement without bargaining with the union. The agreement is very limited and only includes those people that were included in the original certification.

The second version of the recognition clause is like the first, but also includes the specific unit description from the NLRB decision referenced.

The third clause is slightly broader than the first. Instead of using the NLRB decision to define the unit, this clause limits the unit by reference to a schedule attached to the document. As negotiations continue over time the positions included in the schedule can expand, thereby expanding the bargaining unit. There is no attempt in this clause to limit the expansion of the bargaining unit in any way through the original certification. While this clause is less narrow than the first, it could be narrowed through bargaining. Management can presumably limit the bargaining unit under this agreement by eliminating positions that are included in the attached schedule.

The fourth version is even more expansive because it also includes specific language on adding to the unit. This clause provides a process by which those newly created positions will be included in the bargaining unit. Absent language of this nature, a company could argue (particularly if the clause referenced a specific certification decision) that newly created positions were not included in the collective bargaining agreement.

The fifth version includes language on bargaining over revised job descriptions as well as new jobs "within the Union's jurisdiction." This broad clause allows for the expansion of the bargaining unit during the term of the contract. The Union "jurisdiction" language is very dangerous, because jurisdiction could be questioned and expanded during an arbitration. For example, a company might originally recognize a union to cover all "production area employees" while all maintenance functions are performed by a contractor. If the company later decides to perform maintenance in production areas with its own employees the Union could claim that these jobs should now be covered by the bargaining agreement since they are jobs in a "production area" and this is within the Union's jurisdiction.

RECOGNITION (version 1)
The Company recognizes the Union as the sole and exclusive bargaining agent for all full-time and regular part-time production and maintenance employees employed at the Company's facility located at _____, _____, _____, but excluding truck drivers, all clericals, guards and supervisors as defined in the Act and all other employees. Said recognition will be in accordance with the decision of the National Labor Relations Board in _____.

RECOGNITION (version 2)

Section 1. The Company hereby recognizes [Union Name], as the representative for the purposes of collective bargaining with respect to wages, hours, and terms and conditions of employment for all employees included in the bargaining Unit.

Section 2. The bargaining units for which this recognition is accorded is as defined in the certification issued by the National Labor Relations Board, hereinafter also referred to as "NLRB," on [Date], in Case Number [Case No.]. The Unit description in [Case No.] reads as follows:

Unit: Included: All full and regular part-time production employees. Excluded: All office clerical, supervisors and guards as defined in the Act.

RECOGNITION – MEMBERSHIP (version 3)

The Employer recognizes the Union as the exclusive collective bargaining agent in matters pertaining to hours, wages, and other conditions of employment for all production, maintenance, shipping and warehouse employees excluding, however spot and temporary employees as defined in Schedule B attached to and made a part of this agreement.

RECOGNITION (Version 4)

Section 1. The Employer recognizes the Union as the sole and exclusive bargaining representative with respect to hours, wages, terms and conditions of employment for the bargaining unit consisting of the following position classifications: [List Classifications].

Section 2. In the event that the Union seeks to add to the bargaining unit a position classification which may be appropriate to the bargaining unit, the parties agree to meet to discuss the inclusion of the position classification in the bargaining unit. The final determination as to the appropriateness of the inclusion of additional position classifications in the bargaining unit is solely within the jurisdiction of the National Labor Relations Board.

Section 3. The parties agree that the change in title of a position classification in the bargaining unit shall not remove the position classification from the bargaining unit as long as the type of work performed by the position remains essentially the same.

RECOGNITION (Version 5)

The Employer recognizes the Union as sole collective bargaining agents for all employees of the Employer in all classifications contained in Schedule A of this Agreement employed by the Employer at its airports, excluding: supervisors with the power to hire, fire, discipline, reward, responsibly direct or to effectively recommend any of the foregoing; office employees, professionals and employees of contractors or tenants of the Employer. The Employer will send copies to the union of any revised job descriptions for classifications contained in Schedule A of this agreement. Before creating or abolishing any represented classification, the Employer shall notify the Union affected to discuss the effect. Whenever the Employer creates a new position under the jurisdiction of one the Union, and such position is classified under a job title not in Schedule A, the Employer and the Union shall meet within ten (10) days to negotiate a wage scale for the classification. If agreement is not reached, the final wage scale determination will be made within sixty (60) days by a three (3) person panel consisting of one (1)

Employer representative, one (1) Union representative, and one (1) party selected by mutual agreement of the Employer and the Union. The position will not be filled until the wage rate has been determined.

Management Rights

One of the most important clauses in any labor agreement is the management rights clause. Companies use the clause to justify actions not specifically authorized by their labor contract or to defeat grievances that are not based on specific prohibitions in the contract. Unions attempt to negotiate restrictive management right clauses, giving them greater leeway and rights for their members.

As one might gather from the name of the clause, the basic issue negotiated in these clauses is what freedom managers have to make decisions that affect bargaining unit members, without first bargaining with the union, during the term of the labor contract. This clause is supposed to clarify situations where management acts in an area not specifically covered by the contract. Unions obviously hope to limit management freedom to act in all areas, whether specifically covered in the contract or not. For that reason, unions will attempt to negotiate limited management rights language (or reject such language altogether).

The management rights clauses included here range from very broad and favorable clauses for management to narrowly tailored and more favorable ones for unions. The most favorable situation for most unions is to have no management rights clause whatsoever, the implication being that the contract lists management's rights exclusively. Very few collective bargaining agreements do not contain some sort of management rights provision.

Management rights clauses are used to protect

management's right to make decisions during the term of a contract without first bargaining with the union. Most clauses include very broad language protecting management's right to act in any area that is not specifically restricted by the collective bargaining agreement. If management does act in one of these non-restricted areas, unions will sometimes file an unfair labor practice stating that the company refused to bargain over the issue. Management will then rely on the language of the management rights clause to prove that it retained its right to act in the area, without first bargaining with the union, during the term of the collective bargaining agreement.

Provisions of a labor contract limit management's right to act. A core issue in any arbitration case where the defense is a management rights clause is what effect the clause has where ambiguous language limits management's rights elsewhere in the contract. Where there is ambiguity the core question is how expansively to read the protections of the management rights clause. Most arbitrators will read an ambiguous clause in a light most favorable to an employee unless there is clear and unambiguous language expressing that management's right to act in these ambiguous areas is clearly reserved for management. Thus, unions want to limit the management rights language, while companies want it to be broad.

As you can see by looking at the model clauses, each management rights clause includes similar language. However, there are typically compromises in one or more of the following areas:
   ❑   Whether there will be an enumerated list of

"rights" and what is included in that list
- The effect on rights that are not enumerated in the clause (Do they remain with management?)
- Whether items that are covered elsewhere in the agreement can also be included in the enumerated list
- Rights that are most often considered include: subcontracting; establishing work standards and rules; plant closing; staffing requirements (including overtime); promotion
- What effect a specific clause in the contract has on the management rights language
- Whether violations of the management rights pledge is subject to the grievance procedure

Clause Summaries and Drafting Notes

The first clause is rather expansive, enumerating a number of the more controversial rights like the right to subcontract, reduce operations, modify job and staffing requirements and others. The clause is very favorable to management not only because it includes a pretty extensive list of rights, but it also states that these rights are "exclusive" of the company and they are not the only rights protected (it says the rights "include, but are not limited to" the enumerated rights). Further, Section 2 contains interesting language regarding the "common law" management rights that remain with the company after the contract and they are not "waived." The actual effect of such language is not clear, but it certainly seems to indicate that the parties did not intend for the contract to substantially limit management's right to act in the enumerated areas. This is a very strong clause for management.

The second clause is also pretty expansive, although on closer examination it is clearly not as broad or strong as the first. It enumerates a number of the more critical rights listed above (for example, the right to choose plant location, discontinue departments or operations, and to discipline and direct employees). However, some other key rights are not expressed, particularly the right to subcontract work. While there is a clause that states other rights not listed still belong to management, it qualifies this statement by saying these rights are retained to the extent they are "not otherwise specifically restricted by this agreement." Finally, the clause concludes by saying anything listed in the management rights clause should not be interpreted to alter any of the specific provisions of the agreement (and that is the rub – the union presumably only files a grievance when they feel that management is acting inconsistently with their interpretation of the agreement). In my mind this limiting language provides the exception that swallows the rule–overall, I view this clause as being pretty strong for the union.

The third and fourth clauses are somewhat more limited (they each enumerate a smaller number of rights for management), although they more clearly outline the company's right to discontinue operations or eliminate job classifications. Each of these clauses, however, also contain the exception that could swallow the rule. The third clause states that the rights listed are "subject to the terms of this agreement." The fourth clause provides that the management rights clause, "will not be used for the purpose of discrimination against any employee or to avoid any of the provisions of this agreement." As far as they go, these clauses are probably slightly more favorable to management than the second one. However, they each have the same problem of limiting the protection by the terms of the remainder of the agreement.

The fifth clause is interesting. It does contain "limiting" language like clauses three and four, but it seems to reserve more rights to management. In addition, it includes a lengthy list of rights that are quite expansive.

The last two model clauses are more favorable to the union. Although they do enumerate some rights for management, each of them also specifically provides the union with the right to file grievances on behalf of members for violation of the agreement. Although it is understood that, in most contracts, the union has the right to file grievances when it believes the contract has been violated, these clauses clearly associate the grievance process with the management rights clause. This is more favorable to the union.

MANAGEMENT RIGHTS (version 1)
Section 1. The management of its employees, the control of the premises, and the direction of the work force are vested exclusively with the Company and include, but are not limited to the following: the direction of the work force which includes the right to hire, assign, promote, demote, terminate, or transfer employees; to discharge, suspend, or otherwise discipline; to require overtime to work and assign to such work those employees deemed by it most capable; to determine, establish, or modify staffing requirements, job duties, work load, or quality of

workmanship for all classifications; to set standards of efficiency; to relieve employees from duty because of lack of work; to subcontract any work deemed advisable; to promulgate and enforce conduct and working rules and impose penalties for violations thereof; to reduce operations; to plan, direct, change, schedule, and control the operations of the Company and the personnel, methods, equipment, and machinery used in the operation of the Company; to transfer or cease any or all operations of its facility; and to determine the number of hours per day or per week operations shall be carried on. Such rights shall be exclusive to the Company.

Section 2. The parties further understand and agree that all inherent common law management functions and prerogatives which the Company has not waived in this Agreement are retained and vested exclusively in the Company.

MANAGEMENT RIGHTS (Version 2)

The management of the Company and the direction of the working force, including the right to plan, direct and control plant operations; to schedule and assign work to employees; to determine the means, methods, processes, materials, and schedules of production; to determine the products to be manufactured; to choose the location of its plants and the continuance of its operating departments; to establish production standards and to maintain the efficiency of employees; to establish and require employees to observe Company rules and regulations; to hire, layoff or relieve employees from duties ; and to maintain order and to suspend, demote, discipline and discharge employees for just cause, are the recognized reserved rights of the

Company.

The foregoing enumeration of management's rights shall not be deemed to exclude other rights of management not specifically set forth, the Company therefore retaining all rights not otherwise specifically restricted by this agreement. The exercise by the Company of any of the foregoing rights shall not alter any of the specific provisions of this agreement; nor shall they be used to discriminate against any member of the Union or bargaining unit.

MANAGEMENT RIGHTS (version 3)
Section 1. The management of the plant and the direction of the work forces, including the right to hire, discipline, suspend and discharge for just cause, and the right to lay-off employees because of lack of work are exclusive rights and functions of the company subject to the terms of this agreement.
Section 2. The establishment of new jobs, abolishment of or changes in existing jobs, the type of products to be manufactured, the location of the operations, the schedules or restrictions of production, the schedules of work, and the method, process and means of manufacturing are exclusive rights and functions of management subject to the terms of this agreement.

MANAGEMENT RIGHTS (version 4)
The management of the plant and the direction of the working force, including the right to hire, suspend or discharge for cause, to assign to jobs, to transfer employees within the plant, to increase and decrease the working force, to determine products to be handled,

produced or manufactured, the schedules of production and the methods, processes and means of production or handling is vested exclusively in the Employer, provided this will not be used for the purpose of discrimination against any employee or to avoid any of the provisions of this agreement.

MANAGEMENT RIGHTS (version 5)

The Employer continues to retain, whether exercised or not, the sole right to operate and manage its affairs in all respects. Any power or authority, which the Employer has not abridged, delegated or modified by the express provisions of this Agreement, is retained by the Employer. The rights of the Employer, through its management officials, include, but is not limited to, the following:

a) determine the overall budget of the employer;

b) determine control and exercise discretion over the organization and efficiency of operations;

c) direct the employees, including the right to assign work;

d) hire, examine, promote, train and schedule employees in positions with the employer;

e) suspend, demote, discharge, or take other disciplinary action against the employees for proper cause;

f) increase, reduce, change, modify or alter the composition and size of the workforce with proper notification to the local union;

g) set standards for services to the public;

h) change or eliminate existing methods, equipment or facilities;

i) determine the purpose of each of its service areas;

j) determine the locations, methods, means, and personnel by which new or temporary operations are to be conducted, including the right to determine whether goods and services are to be provided or purchased.

MANAGEMENT RIGHTS (version 6)

The Union agrees that the Company has and will continue to retain, whether exercised or not, the right to determine unilaterally the purpose of each of its constituent agencies, set standards of services to be offered to the public, and exercise control and discretion over its organization and operations. It is also the right of the public employer to direct its employees, take disciplinary action for proper cause, and relieve its employees from duty because of lack of work or for other legitimate reasons, except as abridged or modified by the express provisions of this Agreement; provided, however, that the exercise of such rights shall not preclude an employee or employee representative from raising a grievance on any such decision which violates the terms and conditions of this Agreement.

MANAGEMENT RIGHTS (version 7)

Section 1. The right to hire and to maintain order and efficiency is the sole responsibility of the Employer. The right to promote and the right to discipline and discharge for cause are rightfully the sole responsibility of the Employer, provided that claims of wrong and unjust discipline shall be subject to grievance procedure.

Section 2. The Union recognizes other rights and responsibilities belonging solely to the Employer, prominent among them, but by no means wholly inclusive, being the unrestricted rights to instruct its employees as to their normal duties; to regulate methods of production or the kind of machinery, apparatus or equipment used; and to set up the most efficient system of production. In exercising its rights hereunder, the Employer agrees that it will not violate any provision of this Agreement.

Prevailing Rights

This is a unique provision–there is only one example. It could be thought of as an "anti-management rights" clause. Its purpose is essentially to freeze work conditions in time (as they are at the time the contract is entered) and prevent management from changing them during the term of the contract.

Clause Summary and Drafting Notes

The clause included here states that working conditions in place prior to the union's certification as bargaining representative will remain in place during the term of the contract. This clause, unlike a typical management rights clause, prohibits changing any of these terms or conditions without bargaining with the union first. Under the typical management rights clause, as we learned earlier, management reserves the right to make changes in any conditions of employment that are not specifically prohibited by the collective bargaining agreement. This clause reverses that presumption and says that policies and work conditions in place at the time the contract is entered (even if not specifically discussed in the contract) must remain exactly as they are during the term of the contract.

This is obviously a very pro-union clause. Management negotiators should never consider agreeing to such a clause unless they are getting something VERY good in return (maybe an agreement that the union promises to compensate you for any lost sales or increased costs during the term of the agreement). Union negotiators should definitely consider proposing a clause like this, if for no other reason than to put the management rights discussion in context and perhaps to get concessions on the management rights language.

PREVAILING RIGHTS (version 1)
Section 1. All pay and benefits provisions published in the Personnel Rules which cover employees in this bargaining unit and which are not specifically provided for or modified by this Agreement shall continue in effect during the term of this Agreement.

Section 2. Any claim by an employee concerning the application of such provisions shall not be subject to the Grievance Procedure of this Agreement but shall be subject to the method of review prescribed by the Personnel Rules or other appropriate administrative or judicial remedy.

Union Security

Union security is probably the most important provision in a collective bargaining agreement for the union. The union security provision is the one that requires, as a condition of employment, that employees either join the union as members or pay fees to the union in order to remain employed.

The importance of this clause to unions should be self-evident; it ensures that they receive the highest possible revenues from the bargaining unit. It ensures that everyone is required to pay them money in order to be employed—in a non-right-to-work state there is no option. It is often a strike issue for the union.

Companies often resist union security clauses. There are a number of reasons. Pragmatically, these clauses increase the financial strength and control of the union. In addition, since these clauses are so important to unions, companies will often withhold them as bargaining chips during negotiations. Philosophically many employers also resist the clauses because they seem counter to the democratic American principle of freedom of association.

In a right-to-work state these clauses are unenforceable and illegal. Employees in right-to-work states are not required to either join a union or pay fees to a union as a condition of employment. Today there are 22 right-to-work states—to see whether your state is one, check out www.nrtw.org for an updated list. If your company happens to be in a right to work state you should not agree to a union security provision; even if you do, the union security provision would not be enforceable in your state.

In non-right-to-work states union security clauses are lawful. There are several types of union security arrangements:

- ❑ "Closed shops" are companies who require employees to be union members <u>before</u> they can be considered for employment; often these shops only accept employees through a union hiring hall; these kinds of shops are less common today than in years past
- ❑ "Union shops" are the most common; they require employees to either join the union or, in lieu of becoming a member (the Supreme Court says that you cannot be forced to join any organization as a condition of employment) to pay an "agency fee" to the union (or for religious objectors to pay an equal amount to a charity) equal to the share of normal dues that go for "representational" activities
- ❑ "Maintenance of membership" is a type of union security arrangement that gives employees the right to join the union or not (if you don't join the union you don't even have to pay the "agency fee" like you do in a union shop); once you join there are limited circumstances in which you can get out of the union
- ❑ "Open shop" means that there is no requirement to join the union or to pay dues or fees as a condition of employment–this is what you have in right-to-work states, although you can agree to an open shop in any state; employees in an open shop can resign their

membership at any time (although they may be required to continue paying dues or agency fees according to the terms of their dues check-off clause)

Clause Summaries and Drafting Notes

The first version is a normal clause. It contains two security provisions—a "maintenance of membership" provision as well as a "union shop" provision. The maintenance of membership language is probably a remnant of the original collective bargaining agreement, since most employees would be covered by the union shop clause (when the contract was originally entered the company and union apparently agreed to allow employees to not join the union). The "union shop" provision is somewhat typical, although it clearly points out that employees have the option to either join the union and begin paying dues or to execute a check-off authorization to pay an "agency fee" to the union (many clauses do not make the distinction and leave it to employees to figure this out on their own). This clause also contains a statement for religious objectors (another less typical provision) and states clearly that paying the dues or fees is a condition of employment. Insisting on statements regarding agency fee and religious objector status are good strategies for employer drafters.

The second version is even more pro-management, containing a clear "proportionate share fee" statement based on the requirements set forth by the Supreme Court *Communication Workers v. Beck* . It states that employees who choose not to pay dues are required to pay a proportionate share fee for representational activities performed by the union. This clause does state that dues will be taken out of an employee's paycheck (this is a dues check-off clause—you'll see more of these later) and contains a clause requiring the union to indemnify the employer for any mistakes that are made in the enforcement of the dues check-off obligation.

The third version contains a specific clause regarding union membership as opposed to agency fee, contains a fare-share provision and a dues check off provision.

The fourth version is the "anti-union security clause" and is a clear statement that there is no union shop. In other words, employees are not required to join the union or pay fees to the union as a condition of employment. This is the most aggressively pro-management clause and a good starting point for first contract negotiations if you are negotiating on behalf of the company. A clause like this is rarely (if ever) agreed to by a union in a non-right-to-work state.

<u>UNION SECURITY (version 1)</u>

Section 1. An employee employed at the time this Agreement becomes effective who is a member of the Union at such time shall, not later than the fifteenth (15th) calendar day of each calendar month of employment, tender to the Union an amount of money equal to the monthly dues uniformly charged by the Union to all employees who are members of the Union.
Section 2. An employee employed at the time this Agreement becomes effective who is not a member of the Union at such time shall, not later than the thirtieth (30th) day of employment or the effective date of this

Agreement, whichever is later, if still employed, tender to the Union: (i) an amount of money equal to the initiation fee uniformly charged by the Union to all employees who become members of the Union, unless the employee has, at any previous time, tendered such an amount of money to the Union; and (ii) the pro rata share of an amount of money equal to the monthly dues uniformly charged by the Union to all employees who are members of the Union. Thereafter, such an employee shall, not later than the fifteenth (15th) calendar day of each calendar month of employment, tender to the Union an amount of money equal to the monthly dues uniformly charged by the Union to all employees who are members of the Union.

Section 3. An employee who is initially employed or re-employed after the time this Agreement becomes effective shall, not later than thirty (30) calendar days after the commencement of employment, if still employed, tender to the Union: (i) an amount of money equal to the initiation fee uniformly charged by the Union to all employees who become members of the Union, unless the employee has, at any previous time, tendered such an amount of money to the Union; and (ii) the pro rata share of an amount of money equal to the monthly dues uniformly charged by the Union to all employees who are members of the Union. Thereafter, such an employee shall, not later than the fifteenth (15th) calendar day of each calendar month of employment, tender to the Union an amount of money equal to the monthly dues uniformly charged by the Union to all employees who are members of the Union.

Section 4. For purposes of this Agreement, "dues" and "initiation fee" shall encompass only those amounts of money necessary for the Union to perform its duties as the exclusive representative of employees in dealing with the Company on labor-management issues.

Section 5. For the purposes of this Agreement, the "pro rata share" to be tendered to the Union shall be determined by dividing the monthly dues uniformly charged by the Union to all employees who are members of the Union by the total number of days in the month and multiplying the result by the number of days remaining in the calendar month after the employee is required to pay such share.

Section 6. An employee who, because of sincerely held religious beliefs, objects to joining or financially supporting labor organizations shall comply with the provisions of this Agreement in Section 1, 2 or 3, whichever is applicable; except that, in lieu of tendering payment to the Union, such an employee shall pay the amount of monies specified under such paragraphs either to (any of three Subsection 501(c)(3) charities), as selected by the employee. Not later than the end of the first (1st) shift of the first (1st) working day after the tender dates specified in Section 2 or 3, the employee shall deliver to the Union Shop Steward a dated receipt from the charity indicating that payment of the required amount was received by the charity on or before the applicable tender date.

Section 7. The Union may demand the discharge of any employee who, on any tender date specified in Section 1, 2, or 3, fails to comply with the provisions of the Section, by serving written notice thereof on the Company not later than ten (10) calendar days after such tender date, if, prior to such tender date, the Union has notified the employee of the exact amount of the financial obligation due to the Union. As soon as the Company verifies that the employee specified in such written notice failed to comply with the provisions of Section 1, 2, or 3 and that the discharge of the employee would not otherwise be unlawful, the Company shall discharge the employee.

UNION SECURITY (version 2)
Section 1. Upon this provision taking effect, the Union shall submit to the Employer an affidavit which certifies the amount constituting an Employee's proportionate share of the cost of the collective bargaining process, initiation fees and the contract administration, which amount shall not in any event exceed the dues uniformly required of members of the Union.

Section 2. The proportionate share fee deduction shall commence with the first pay period starting 30 days after the Union certifies to the Employer the amount of the proportionate share fee, or 30 days after the date of original employment for a new employee, whichever is later. Each full-time employee in the bargaining unit who is not a member of the Union shall be required to pay the proportionate share fee. Such proportionate share payments shall be deducted from the earnings of the non-member full-time employees pursuant to usual and customary payroll deduction procedures and paid to the union.

Section 3. The Employer agrees to deduct Union dues, assessments, and Union sponsored benefit program contributions from the pay of those employees who are Union members covered by this Agreement and who individually, on a form provided by the Union, request in writing that such deductions are made. The Union shall certify the current amount of Union deductions.

Section 4. The amount of the above employee deductions shall be remitted to [Union Name] after the deduction is made by the Employer with a listing of each employee, social security number, and the individual employee deduction(s).

Section 5. The Union shall indemnify and hold harmless the Employer, its officers, agents and employees from and against any and all claims, demands, actions, complaints, suits or other forms of liability that shall arise out of or by reasons of action taken by the Employer for the purposes of complying with the above provisions of this clause or in reliance on any list, notice, certification, affidavit or assignment furnished.

UNION SECURITY (version 3)

Section 1 - Union Membership. All employees covered by this Agreement shall within thirty-one (31) days of employment either (1) become and remain a member of the Union or (2) tender to the Union a fair share equivalent to regular union dues, initiation fees, and assessments, if any. If the employee is a member of a church or religious body which has bona fide religious tenets or teachings which prohibit such employees from being a member of or contributing to a labor organization, such employee shall pay an amount of money equivalent to regular union dues and initiation fees and assessments, if any, to a nonreligious charity or to another charitable organization mutually agreed upon by the employee and the Union. The employee shall furnish written proof to the Employer that this has been done.

Section 2 - Fair Share Payments. Fair share payments authorized by this Article shall be deducted by the Employer. The Union assumes responsibility for repayment of monies found to be erroneously deducted by the Employer under this Article.

Section 3 - Union Dues Check-off. The Employer will provide for Union dues check-off through payroll deduction in providing payroll deduction for dues by the Employer. The performance of these services is at no cost to the Unions.

UNION SECURITY (language expressly saying no union shop) (version 4)

The Union and the Company agree that whether an employee belongs to the Union or doesn't belong to the Union is a matter of personal choice for each individual employee. Employees do not have to belong to the Union or pay a fee to the Union in order to work at the Company.

UNION SECURITY (Fair Share language and language saying no union shop) (version 5)

Section 1. Membership Not Required.
Membership in any Employee organization is not compulsory. Employees have the right to join, not join, maintain or drop their membership in any Employee organization as they see fit.

Section 2. Dues Deduction. The Employer agrees that it will deduct from the monthly earnings of all Employees in the collective bargaining unit, the amount of the monthly dues certified by the Union as the current dues uniformly required of all members, and pay said amount to the treasurer of the Union on or before the end of the month in which such deduction was made.

Section 3. Changes In Amount. Changes in the amount of dues to be deducted shall be certified by the Union 30 days before the effective date of the change.

Section 4. New Employees. As to new employees, such deductions shall be made from the first paycheck following the first six (6) months of employment.

Dues Check-off

A close cousin to the union security clause, the dues check-off provision is the second most important clause unions insist upon in labor contracts. The dues check-off provision states that the company will, as part of its normal payroll process, deduct dues, initiation fees, assessments and other payments to the union out of an employee's regular paycheck before issuing that paycheck to the employee. In essence the company becomes the collection arm for the labor organization.

There are several key interests at stake when negotiating the dues check-off provision. Unlike the union security provision, the company is agreeing to perform an administrative function for the union so there is some cost involved with administering the dues check-off provision. Companies also want protection from potential liability for improper deductions, since they must rely on the union for information about the correct amounts to deduct. Additionally the company may want to keep responsibility for dues collection on the part of the union since it is much more difficult for the union to collect funds once they get into the pockets of members; disgruntled or financially strapped members are unlikely to write that monthly check to the union if they can avoid it.

Unions have important interests in getting the company to agree to a dues check-off provision. Unions simply do not want to have to show up, hat in hand, each month to collect dues from members. It is just easier to collect the dues at the point of the initial paycheck than to do so after the money is received by members; there is one collection point instead of hundreds or even thousands. Since most employers already have a computerized system to handle payroll deductions the actual cost of dues check-off for the employer is minimal. Dues check-off frees up the union's limited administrative resources to spend on more important day-to-day functions like handling grievances or organizing.

Unions will bargain for the dues check-off compromise as hard as they do for the union security one—it is normally a deal-breaker. For this reason, smart company negotiators will use the union security and dues check-off compromise as late "bargaining chips." Unions are used to this strategy, and also know that ultimately these compromises typically mean much less to the company than they do to the union. Therefore, the company position on the issue must be principled and well-communicated if it is to be taken seriously by the union.

Clause Summaries and Drafting Notes
As you have seen in the earlier provisions, some companies and unions agree to use check-off language as part of their union security clause. Other contracts contain a separate clause on dues check-off. The first version contains standard check-off authorization. One additional protection that is less common (but very reasonable in my view) is the language that requires the union to collect dues or fees from any employee whose paycheck would go into a negative balance. In addition, there is an indemnification clause for the company that protects it from lawsuits by employees as well as tax-related litigation. This type of language is more common. Finally, this clause contains a specific

form for the check-off authorization (included as an appendix to the contract). This is a good idea to make sure that the authorization language is agreed upon by both the company and the union before it is enforced.

The second version includes the basic check-off authorization language along with several other provisions. Like version one, it includes a provision on no negative balances. It also includes language requiring the union to reimburse employees for whom improper deductions are made, as well as indemnification for the employer for improper deductions. This clause also contains a specific form for the check-off authorization (included as an appendix to the contract).

The third version really isn't a dues check-off clause at all. Instead it is language referring to members' *Beck* rights; this is aggressive language most favorable to companies. It would most likely be proposed by the company to "tweak" the union negotiating team. This clause contains a specific reference to the Supreme Court's decision in *Communication Workers vs. Beck* and requires the union to provide proof of the way that it determined the "proportional fee" to be paid by *Beck* objectors. It also requires the union to inform members of their *Beck* rights on an annual basis.

DUES CHECK-OFF (version 1)
Section 1. Upon receipt by the Company of a check-off authorization in the form set forth in Section 2 of this Agreement, dated and executed by an employee, the Company shall deduct, from the wages owed such employee for the first payroll period ending in each

calendar month following receipt of such check-off authorization, until such check-off authorization is revoked by the employee in accordance with the terms thereof, the Union's membership dues for the month in which such deduction is made. The Company will forward the monies so deducted to the Treasurer of the Union not later than the fifteenth (15th) day of the calendar month in which the deduction is made. The Company shall deduct from an employee's wages only that amount of money which the Treasurer of the Union has certified to the Company, in writing, is the amount of dues, properly established by the Union in accordance with applicable law and the Union's constitution and bylaws, required of all employees as a condition of acquiring or retaining membership in the Union. If, for any payroll period in which the Company is obligated to make deductions, the wages owed an employee (after deductions mandated by any governmental body) are less than the amount of money which the employee has authorized the Company to deduct, the Company shall make no deductions, from wages owed the employee for that payroll period and shall make no deductions, which would have been made from wages owed the employee for that payroll period, from wages owed the employee for any future payroll period.

Section 2. The Company shall not deduct any monies from an employee's wages pursuant to Section 1 of this Agreement, unless the check-off authorization executed by the employee conforms exactly to the following form:

CHECK-OFF AUTHORIZATION

I hereby authorize _____ to deduct from wages owed to me for the first payroll period ending in each calendar month, and to forward to _____, the monthly membership dues uniformly required of all employees as a condition of acquiring or retaining membership in _____. This check-off Authorization shall be irrevocable for a period of one year following my execution thereof, or until the expiration of any applicable collective bargaining agreement, whichever occurs sooner. Thereafter, it shall be automatically renewed for successive one (1) year periods unless written notice of revocation of this Check-off Authorization, executed by me, is delivered to _____: (1) during the period commencing thirty (30) days prior to and ending five (5) days prior to (a) the annual anniversary of my execution hereof, or (b) the expiration date of any collective bargaining agreement obligating _____ to honor this Check-off Authorization, or (2) during any period when there is no collective bargaining agreement in effect obligating _____ to honor this Check-off Authorization. (Dated and Signed by Employee).

Section 3. The Union shall defend, indemnify, and save the Company harmless against any claims, demands, suits, grievances, or other liability (including attorneys' fees incurred by the Company) that arise out of or by reason of actions taken by the Company pursuant to this Article ___.

Dues Check-off (Version 2)

Section 1. During the term of this Agreement, the Company agrees to deduct membership dues and uniform assessments, if any, in an amount established by the Union and certified in writing by the President of the Union to the Company, from the pay of those employees in the bargaining units who individually make such request on a written check-off authorization form provided by the Union (Appendix B). Such deduction will be made by the Company when other payroll deductions are made and will begin with the pay for the first full pay period following receipt of the authorization by the Company. The Association shall advise the Company of any uniform assessment or increase in dues in writing at least thirty (30) days prior to its effective date. This Article applies only to the deduction of membership dues and uniform assessments, if any, and shall not apply to the collection of any fines, penalties, or special assessments. Employee organization dues deduction will be provided for the certified bargaining agent only.

Section 2. Deductions of dues and uniform assessments, if any, shall be remitted exclusively to the President of the Union, or his designee, by the Company on either a biweekly or monthly cycle along with a list containing names, social security numbers, and amount deducted, of the employees for whom the remittance is made.

Section 3. In the event an employee's salary earnings within any pay period, after deductions for withholding, social security, retirement, and insurance, are not sufficient to cover dues and any uniform assessments, it will be the responsibility of the Union to collect its dues and uniform assessments for that pay period directly from the employee.

Section 4. Deductions for Union dues and/or uniform assessments shall continue until either: (1) revoked by the employee by providing the Company and the Union with thirty (30) days written notice that he is terminating the prior check-off authorization; (2) the termination of employment; or (3) the transfer, promotion, or demotion of the employee out of this bargaining unit. If these deductions are continued when any of the above situations occur, the Union shall, upon notice of the error, reimburse the employee for the deductions that were improperly withheld.

Section 5. The Union shall indemnify, defend and hold the Company, its officers, officials, agents and employees, harmless against any claim, demand, suit, or liability (monetary or otherwise) and for all legal costs arising from any action taken or not taken by the Company, its officials, agents, and employees in complying with this Article. The Union shall promptly refund to the Company any funds received in accordance with this Article which are in excess of the amount of dues and/or uniform assessments which the Company or its agencies have agreed to deduct.

Section 6. The Dues Check-off Authorization Form (Appendix B) supplied by the Union shall: (1) be in strict conformance with Appendix B; (2) be the only form used by bargaining unit employees who wish to initiate dues deduction; (3) contain all the information required for processing prior to submission to the Company. Changes in the Dues Check-off Authorization Form will not affect deductions authorized by forms that the parties have previously agreed to.

LANGUAGE RE *BECK* DECISION

As used in this Article, the phrase "member of the Union" shall include "financial core" membership. Fees for "financial core" members will not include dues or other amounts that will be spent for purposes unrelated to the collective bargaining, contract administration or grievance adjustment. For the purpose of this Article, said dues or other amounts shall be referred to as "representational share". The "representational share" will be determined in accord with the decision of the Supreme Court of the United States in *Communication Workers v. Beck*, 128 LRRM 2729 (1988). The Union will disclose the necessary information so as to assure that the proportionate "representational share" may be properly calculated. The Union will inform members of their *Beck* rights on an annual basis through a paycheck notification during the first pay period each year.

Union Representation

These "catch all" provisions cover basic union administration issues. The basic purpose of these clauses is to protect the union's right to represent employees within the bargaining unit. The main competing interests involved in negotiating these clauses are:

- ❏ The property rights of the employer
- ❏ The right of the employer to manage and control the daily operations of the business
- ❏ The right of the union to meet with, communicate with and otherwise represent members

Compromises regarding these interests primarily cover issues like the union's right for access to the property (and the circumstances under which this permission may be denied), the right to communicate through bulletin boards, and the right to represent employees in grievances. The employer typically wants to ensure that it retains some control over the union's access to members, particularly in work areas and during work time. The union wants as expansive rights to access as the employer is willing to grant.

Clause Summaries and Drafting Notes

There are three examples of union representation clauses here. As discussed above, these are "catch all" provisions in many contracts, so there are any number of additional issues that could be proposed depending on the specific circumstances of a particular negotiation.

The first version contains a provision that provides a union steward for each shift. It also ensures that the union stewards are given access to the property and to employees for the purpose of investigating grievances and conducting grievance meetings. The clause does provide that these meetings will only occur outside of regular working hours. It also provides for the use of a bulletin board. This language is relatively favorable for management.

The second model union representation clause is more favorable to the union. It requires the employer to give access to the property for union representatives, although it requires them to apply for permission to management before they are provided access. It does say that union representatives will not interfere with company business, but it does not state under what conditions the company may deny access to the union. It contains a statement that there will be no discrimination against union representatives and a clause giving union stewards "super seniority" over others in the bargaining unit. These are very favorable clauses to the union. The clause also requires the union to give the employers the names of stewards, presumably so the employer can administer the other aspects of the clause.

The third version contains another version of a bulletin board access provision as well as a property access provision for union representatives. The property access language is very favorable for the union, allowing access at "all reasonable times" with the only caveat being that the union will not "unreasonably delay" company operations, whatever that might mean. The clause is not artfully drafted. While it clearly provides union access to work areas, and also contemplates that this access will interfere with or delay company business, the job of figuring out whether access or delays are "reasonable" is left to an arbitrator.

UNION REPRESENTATION (version 1)
Section 1. In the administration of this Agreement, the Union shall be represented by a Steward, who shall be a present employee of the Company.
Section 2. In the event that the Company has a second or third shift, the Union may appoint a Steward for each shift. The Union shall advise the Company in writing of the name of the Steward(s).
Section 3. Stewards shall enter and remain in the plant only on their respective shifts.
Section 4. All grievance and negotiating meetings shall take place outside of the regular working hours unless otherwise agreed to by the Company. The parties specifically understand and agree time spent in said meetings shall not be compensated for by the Company.
Section 5. The Company will provide a bulletin board for the exclusive use of the Union. The use of said bulletin board will be limited to official Union business and notices of Union meetings. All notices must be approved by the Plant Manager or someone designated by him prior to posting.

UNION REPRESENTATION (version 2)
Section 1 – Access. The business representative of the various crafts shall have access to the Employer's property by applying for permission through the designated office, provided they do not interfere with or cause workers to neglect their work. Business

representatives shall obey all rules and regulations of the installation.

Section 2 – No Discrimination. The Employer will not in any way discriminate against any shop steward for presenting any complaint, dispute or grievance to the employee's supervisor or department head or to the Human Resources Department in the manner provided for in this Agreement.

Section 3 – Seniority. The shop steward shall have seniority over other employees within the steward's classification during the steward's term of office in regard to layoff and recall.

Section 4. The Union shall advise the Employer of the names of shop stewards currently elected or appointed. The full grievance procedure shall be available to any Union which feels that its shop stewards have been discriminated against.

UNION REPRESENTATION (version 3)

Section 1. The Employer agrees to furnish bulletin board space adjacent to lockers in the shop area for the posting of Union notices related to regular Union business. Such notices shall not be political or partisan in nature and shall not defame the Employer or any individual employed by the Employer. While not limited to the following, notices shall be such as: Union meetings, Union elections, and appointments, results of Union elections, recreational, social and educational programs. All posted notices shall be signed by an officer of the Union.

Section 2. Authorized representatives of the Union shall have access to the Employer's establishment at all reasonable times for the purpose of adjusting disputes, investigating working conditions and ascertaining compliance with this agreement. The Union agrees not to unreasonably delay employees during working hours.

Hiring

Some union contracts include provisions regarding hiring halls or the way the companies hire employees. These are less common in most labor contracts today– hiring halls are more of a remnant of the building and construction trades. However, you can still find them, and one example clause is included here.

The core issue of the compromise on hiring is who will control the hiring process. There are several core aspects of the process that are debated:

- ❑ Sourcing (i.e. will the candidates come from a hiring hall, union referrals, temporary agencies, off the street, etc.)
- ❑ The application process
- ❑ Pre-hiring requirements (including physical exams)
- ❑ The weight given to union membership or recommendations
- ❑ Non-discrimination (most contain a specific provision that union members will receive an equal opportunity for hiring).

Companies will attempt to retain complete control over the hiring process, avoiding any obligation to use hiring halls or give union referrals any preference over outside candidates. Given the numerous restrictions on pre-employment inquiries by employers under civil rights statutes, employers have good reason to keep their hiring process within their control. Unions, of course, want to provide good jobs for their members and attempt to accomplish that through some measure of control in the hiring process.

Clause Summaries and Drafting Notes

There is only one example of a hiring provision from a collective bargaining agreement below. This provision gives the company the right to reject referrals from the union, but also states that the company will give the union applicants an equal opportunity for hiring. It has a provision regarding the requirement that union applicants fill out the same employment records and forms that are required by non-union applicants. It requires union applicants to submit to physical exams. It also includes a 6-month introductory or probationary period for all applicants from union referral sources.

This clause is pretty favorable to management, retaining most of its managerial right to control the hiring process. It does, however, provide the union the right to challenge whether union referred applicants are receiving equal treatment, which can be arbitrated under the contract.

HIRING (version 1)

Section 1. The Employer retains the right to reject any job applicant referred by the Union. The Employer may discharge any employee for just and sufficient cause.

Section 2. Applicant Priority. When hiring additional employees, the Employer shall give equal opportunity to the Union, along with other sources, to provide applicants, provided, however, that when a position is open, existing employees will be given priority over "outside" applicants, provided they meet the position requirements.

Section 3. Records. All employees referred to the Employer by the Union under this article shall submit to the making of such records as are or may be required by the Employer for personnel administration.

Section 4. Physical Examinations. The Employer may also require a physical examination prior to or within the first thirty (30) days of employment. This examination shall be by a physician of the Employer's choice and shall be at the Employer's expense. The Employer agrees to defend and hold harmless the Union, its officers and agents from any liability arising out of the application or administration of this provision.

Section 5 - Introductory Period A period of six (6) months for persons newly employed by the Employer shall constitute an introductory period during which the Employer shall have the right to discharge without any limitations by the Union or this Agreement.

Wages

The wage provisions in labor contracts are about as varied as the companies and unions who enter them. They can be a simple listing of the job classifications along with a minimum, mid-point and maximum point of the range or simple "across-the-board" or "cost of living" increases. They can be much more complex, including production bonuses, gain sharing or profit sharing, differentials and many other variable pay structures.

In addition to the total labor costs for the employer and the total compensation for union members, there are a number of key issues that form the basis of the wage compromise in labor agreements:

- ❑ Most fundamentally, <u>what</u> is compensated–are pay increases based on individual productivity (piece rates, for example), skill level, seniority, plant productivity, inflation or any combination of these or other factors?
- ❑ Equality in the marketplace–i.e. how do wage levels compare to similar employers in the same labor market (or even in different labor markets)?
- ❑ Equality within the company–i.e. how do wage levels compare between classifications in the same organization?
- ❑ Equality within classifications–i.e. is there wage compression between long-term employees, should some employees be "red-lined"?
- ❑ Administration of the increase–percentage increases (these move all employees equally), lump sums (these control future costs and more heavily favor lower-paid employees),

classification-by-classification adjustments
(which can often raise questions about fairness),
at-risk pay (like bonuses based on productivity)
Depending on the organization, there may be many
other factors to consider when making the wage
compromise.

Clause Summaries and Drafting Notes

It is impossible to provide anything approaching a
comprehensive sampling of wage contract clauses since
these provisions are so complex and unique to each
situation. I provide three examples from the most
simple to a more complex version. However, it is
beyond the scope of this book (and probably beyond
the scope of any book) to provide examples of all the
different variations of pay systems that are available.

The first version is the simplest wage provision
possible, stating that wages will be paid per a schedule
or appendix attached to the agreement. This is the
most common type of wage provision. Obviously, the
devil is in the details; the items in the schedule dictate
how pay will be handled in the organization.

The second version references a schedule like version
one, but also discusses a variety of other issues. For
example, there is a lump sum payment provision.
Lump sums are often included as inducements for
people to sign the contract (a "signing bonus"). They
also are used to keep wage levels in line, since the lump
sum is not added into the base wage rate and therefore
does not carry over into future years. There is also a
differential, which is common in multiple shift
operations.

The second version also includes re-opener language. This gives the union the right to ask for the contract to be re-opened during the term of the collective bargaining agreement for negotiation of additional issues regarding wages. In most cases a collective bargaining agreement is not subject to additional negotiations once the parties have made a final agreement. This type of language is most often included in agreements when the parties are having trouble reaching agreement on an issue, normally due to divergent opinions about business conditions in the future. Re-opener language allows the parties to agree on most items "for now" while leaving open the unresolved issues for future negotiating sessions. While this language is useful, it really just puts off difficult issues for the future. This may or may not be in the best interests of long-term labor peace.

The third version is an example of a more complicated wage provision. It contains a percentage increase with a minimum raise for employees who, after receiving the percentage increase, do not reach the minimum. In addition, there is a lump sum provided for employees that have reached the maximum of their wage range. There is a provision for pro-rated pay increases for part-time and temporary employees. There is also a performance component that provides low performing employees with no wage increases until their performance improves. These are more creative and well-designed provisions that attempt to tie pay increases to individual performance. The lump sum and minimum increase provisions are designed to prevent compression on the one hand, while also insuring that employees on both ends of the spectrum do not fall too far behind or get too far ahead of market rates for the jobs performed.

WAGES (version 1)
Wages shall be paid as set forth in Appendix "_____" attached hereto and made a part of this Agreement.

WAGES (version 2)
Section 1. Salary Increase
    A.   The parties agree to the following range of rates for the period of July 1, 2001 through June 30, 2002. [List Rates]

    B.   Upon ratification and approval by both parties, all employees represented by this agreement shall receive a lump sum payment of [Insert Amount].

Section 2. Shift Differential. Any employee, whose regular work schedule makes him/her eligible for payment of a shift differential during 60% or more of their hours in pay status, shall be paid that shift differential for all hours in pay status.

Section 3. Salary Increase – FY2003 & FY2004. For the second and third subsequent fiscal year of this Agreement (FY2003, FY2004), the Company will increase the salary ranges defined in Section 1(A) of this paragraph and the current individual employee rates by [Insert Percentage Increase Amount]. These increases shall be effective July 1 of each subsequent fiscal year.

Section 4. Wage Re-openers – FY2005 & FY2006. There shall be wage re-openers for FY2005 and FY2006, effective July 1, 2004 and July 1, 2005.

Negotiations for these wage re-openers shall commence no later than thirty (30) days prior to July 1, 2004 and July 1, 2005.

WAGES (version 3)
Section 1. General Wage Increase for Fiscal Year 2002-2003

(A) Effective October 1, 2002, each full-time employee shall receive a competitive pay adjustment of 2.5 percent to the employee's September 30, 2002 base rate of pay (exclusive of any salary additives), as appropriate. Each eligible full-time employee shall receive an annualized minimum increase of $600. If the competitive pay adjustment is less than $600, each employee shall receive an additional increase which provides the employee a total annualized increase of $600.

(B) If any portion of the above-specified increase causes an employee's base rate of pay to exceed the adjusted maximum of the pay range for their class/occupational level, the employee's salary will be increased to the adjusted maximum and the portion of the increase that exceeds the maximum shall be granted in a one-time, lump sum payment equal to three-fourths the difference between the adjusted maximum and 2.5 percent of the employee's September 30, 2002 annual base rate of pay.

(C) If an employee's base rate of pay exceeds the adjusted maximum of the pay range, the employee will be granted a one-time lump sum payment in an amount equal to three-fourths of 2.5 percent of their September 30, 2002, annual base rate of pay.

(D) Eligible part-time employees shall receive the applicable salary increase payment effective October 1, 2002, except the increase will be prorated based on the full-time equivalency of the employee's position.

(E) An employee on leave without pay on October 1, 2002, shall receive the October 1, 2002, increase effective the date the employee returns to pay status. In no case shall the increase be retroactive.

(F) An employee whose job performance is unsatisfactory on October 1, 2002, shall receive the increase when the employee's job performance returns to a satisfactory level. In no case shall the increase be retroactive.

(G) The minimum and maximum of each pay grade will be adjusted upward by 2.5 percent, effective October 1, 2002.

Job Rate Changes

Contracts sometimes contain provisions that deal with job changes and/or rate changes during the term of the collective bargaining agreement. Sometimes significant changes occur to the job duties required of somebody already in the bargaining unit during the term of the contract. Other times changes in the company's business require creation of new positions. The parties must have some way to determine how the wages and working conditions of these new or modified positions will be handled.

Companies will argue that such changes fall under the purview of the management rights clause and that the union has no right to challenge the wages and work conditions established by the company, at least until the next round of contract negotiations. Unions will normally reject this line of reasoning, arguing that they will be required to represent these workers and that they have a legal right to bargain over the terms and conditions of their employment.

Instead of waiting for the issue to come up before figuring out how to respond, some companies and unions attempt to handle this up front, through their contract language. Unions will attempt to negotiate language to keep management from going around the collective bargaining agreement by adding additional positions or reassigning tasks within job positions described in the contract. The union wants to make sure that the company cannot get around pay increase provisions, for example, by agreeing to them but then assigning additional duties to employees to require them to perform more work for the money they receive.

Usually these cases are handled with re-opener language. Such clauses simply state that whenever a change like this occurs the company and the union will sit down at that time and bargain over the rate of pay and job responsibilities for the new classification. However, other contracts include more specific language about how these changes will occur. The key issues in the compromise are the company's right to set the terms and conditions of employment (its management rights authority and flexibility to deal with unforeseen changes during the term of a contract) and the union's right to represent all members of the bargaining unit (and its right to insist that management bargain before unilaterally implementing changes in the work conditions of employees).

Clause Summaries and Drafting Notes
There are four versions of job rate change clauses below. The first version provides that there will only be negotiations if there is a "substantial" change in equipment or work method. It protects piece rate changes for bargaining unit employees during the term of the contract by making clear that productivity improvements based on equipment changes or employee effort will not result in rate adjustments. This is strong language in favor of the union and poorly drafted from the standpoint of management. Obviously, the first difficult question to answer is what constitutes a significant substantial change–that is not defined at all in this clause. Since it may be difficult to parse out when productivity improvements are a result of "equipment change" or "employee effort" there is also little incentive for the company to make technology

improvements during the term of the agreement.

The second version states that any new classification is subject to negotiation. This clause essentially puts off any discussion of this until the classification is actually created. The key to this clause is that if the company and the union cannot reach an agreement on the new classification, the change is subject to the arbitration procedure. Further, it states that there will be no economic loss due to changes in classifications during the term of the agreement, which is essentially a "red-line" provision for current employees. Again, this is a pretty strong clause for unions.

The third version requires the company to keep members informed about the classifications in the company. It also requires the company to notify the union if there is any change to classifications during the term of the contract. If the union fails to demand bargaining after being notified of the change, there is a waiver provision. This clause does not deal with the situation where the company creates a new position that may or may not be part of the current bargaining unit.

The fourth version gives employees the right to request review of their position if they believe that they are being asked to do things that are not included in their job requirements. It commits that the company will review their request within 60 days. It does provide, however, that the decision of the plant manager will be final and that is not subject to the grievance procedure. Overall this is a reasonable balance between the concerns of the company and the union, although ultimately it is most favorable to the company since its decision is final and not subject to the grievance procedure.

JOB AND RATE CHANGES (version 1)

Piece work rates in effect and all new or changed piece rates, after having become permanent, will not be changed unless substantial changes occur in equipment, method, or material. A rate shall be considered permanent after having been worked for a reasonable period after being set. Those parts of an operation affected by a substantial change in equipment, method, or material shall be retimed and the part of the piece work rate applicable to that part shall be set to yield not less than 130% of the incentive base rate. Time standards shall not be changed because of the efficiency of, or effort expended by, an employee.

JOB AND RATE CHANGES (version 2)

Section 1. If the Company establishes new classifications, or revises existing classifications to a significant degree, the rate for the new or revised classification will be subject to negotiation. If no agreement is reached, the Company may assign a temporary rate of pay. If the matter remains unresolved for a period of thirty (30) days the temporarily assigned rate will become the accepted rate of the job, unless the Union requests that the matter be processed through arbitration prior to the expiration of the thirty (30) day period.

Section 2. Employees covered by this Agreement receiving higher wages or more attractive working conditions than those provided for in this Agreement shall suffer no reduction by virtue of this Agreement and shall be paid all increases in wages negotiated herein.

JOB AND RATE CHANGES (version 3)
Section 1. The Company will maintain on the Internet the classification specifications and the Personnel Rules which it has published, and which affect employees within the bargaining Unit.
Section 2. In instances where the Company determines that a revision to a class specification or occupational level for positions covered by this Agreement is needed, the Department of Human Resources shall notify the Union in writing of the proposed changes. This procedure shall not constitute a waiver of the Union's right to bargain over such matters. The Union shall notify the Department of Human Resources, in writing within seven (7) calendar days of any comments it has concerning the proposed changes, or of its desire to discuss the proposed change(s). Failure of the Union to notify the Department of Human Resources within this specified period shall constitute a waiver of the right to discuss the change(s).

JOB AND RATE CHANGES (version 4)
Section 1. When an employee alleges that the employee is being regularly required to perform duties which are not included in the position description of the position being filled by the employee, and the employee alleges that the duties assigned are not included in the official class specification to which the position is allocated, the employee may request in

writing that the Director of Human Resources review the duties assigned to the employee's position. The Director of Human Resources or his designee shall review the duties as requested. The employee will receive a copy of the written decision within sixty (60) days of the request. If the decision is that the duties assigned are sufficient to justify reclassifying the position, either the position will be reclassified or the duties in question will be removed. Shortage of funds shall not be used as the basis for refusing to reclassify a position after a review has been completed.

Section 2. If the employee is not satisfied with the decision, the employee, with or without representation, may request in writing a review by the Secretary of the Plant Manager or its designee.

Section 3. The written decision of the Plant Manager or its designee as to the classification of the position shall be final and binding on all parties.

Lunch Period
Companies and unions will often reach some sort of an agreement on breaks or lunch periods. Federal law does not require the company to provide breaks or lunch periods. Although many state laws do require employers to provide lunch periods, most of these laws create exceptions for labor agreements.

The primary interests at stake here are company flexibility on the one hand and the interest of employees in getting rest during their shift on the other.

Clause Summaries and Drafting Notes
Three model clauses are provided. The first is a simple lunch break clause that provides for a one-hour break during an overtime shift in which an employee works four hours or more (not during a regular shift). It gives the employer the option to not provide a meal if it pays the employee $1.50 in lieu of a meal. This is a relatively favorable clause for the company (it only applies for overtime situations), although the time paid for the lunch will be at time and one-half.

The second clause just states that a break will be provided when someone is scheduled for a shift and that it will happen after the first 4 hours of the shift. This again gives management a good amount of flexibility. The company could tighten up this clause by clarifying that the lunch period is unpaid.

The third lunch clause also covers lunch and break periods when an employee is asked to work overtime (once again nothing is said about lunch periods during normal shifts). In this case the break must be provided at the end of the first 8-hour shift and the lunch break will be paid at the overtime rate.

LUNCH PERIOD (version 1)
Employees held over four or more hours overtime consecutive with their regularly scheduled work shift shall receive one hour for lunch with pay. The company also agrees to furnish such held-over employees a meal or, at company's option, allow one dollar and fifty cents ($1.50) in lieu thereof.

LUNCH PERIOD (version 2)
To be taken between the start of the fourth hour and the end of the fifth hour or as close as practicable due to schedule.

LUNCH PERIOD (version 3)
Section 1. A thirty (30) minute lunch period shall be allowed on the Employer's time at the end of the regular shift if employees are required to work overtime in excess of two (2) hours. A meal period shall be allowed on the Employer's time when employees are required to work more than two (2) hours before their regular shift and continue working into their regular shift thereafter.
Section 2. Employees working overtime shall receive a lunch period of thirty (30) minutes on Employer's time every four (4) hours.
Section 3. Section 2 shall not apply to the noon lunch period on Saturdays, Sundays and holidays.
Section 4. Employees required to work during their lunch period shall receive the established overtime rate for such lunch period and shall thereafter be allowed a

reasonable opportunity to eat lunch on the Employer's time.

Call Back Pay

Call back pay is designed to compensate an employee for situations when they are asked to return to the plant when they are off work. There are several issues behind these clauses:

- ❑ The management right to schedule employees according to business needs or call them in to work outside of their regular schedule.
- ❑ To discourage the employer from calling in employees who are off work unless they are certain they will need the employees.
- ❑ To compensate employees for the disruption that can be caused by being called back in when they are either not scheduled or on a holiday or their day off.

Clause Summaries and Drafting Notes

Three examples of how companies and unions handle the issue of call back pay are provided below. The first version is a simple clause that provides that the employer will pay a minimum of two hours pay when an employee is called in and that those two hours will be paid at time and a half the regular rate. It further provides that if an employee is on his or her day off that they will be paid a minimum of four hours pay at time and a half. The first part of that provision would deal with situations where an employee is asked to stay after their regular shift whereas the second part deals with situations where an employee is asked to come in on a day that they are not scheduled.

The second version deals with both call back pay (a minimum of 2 hours when an employee is called back) and on-call pay. In the information age it is becoming extremely common for employees to remain in contact either by cell phone or pager. This provision compensates employees for the time that they are "on-call" and subject to being called in to work at any time. Since the rate of pay for "on-call" assignments are only $24 a day, this clause probably does not significantly restrict the use of "on-call" by the employer. The use of "on-call" assignments on Saturday, Sunday or on holidays may be a little less (since it is paid at a higher rate).

The third version is the most extensive clause, and probably the most favorable to the union. It provides for a minimum of 4 hours of work or 2 hours at double pay if the employee is called in to work on their day off. In addition, it provides "pager pay" of two hour's pay for days the employee is on call. It also provides for overtime pay to begin with the time that the employee leaves their home for work on days when there is ice and snow and travel conditions are difficult, as opposed to the normal rules which state that the overtime pay would begin once the employee clocks in at the plant.

CALL BACK PAY (version 1)
Section 1. An employee who is called back to work after completing a regular day's work shall receive a minimum of two (2) hours pay at one and one-half times the regular rate of pay. An employee called back on a scheduled day off shall receive a minimum of four (4) hours pay at one and one-half times the regular rate of pay.
Section 2. Four hours guaranteed if called to work and sent home on arrival due to cancellation of trip or foul weather.

CALL BACK PAY (version 2)
Section 1 - On-Call Fee.
(A)   When approved as provided herein, an employee who is required to be on-call shall be compensated by payment of a fee in an amount of one dollar ($1.00) per hour for each hour such employee is required to be on-call. If an on-call period is less than one (1) hour, the time while on-call will be rounded to the nearest 1/4 hour and the employee will be paid twenty-five cents (.25) for each 1/4 hour of on-call assignment.
(B)   An employee who is required to be on-call on a Saturday, Sunday, or holiday, will be compensated by payment of a fee in an amount equal to one-fourth (1/4) of the minimum for the employee's class or at the rate specified in the above paragraph, whichever is greater, for each eight (8) hour period such employee is required to be available.
Section 2 - Call-Back. An employee called back to work beyond the employee's scheduled hours of work for that day, shall be credited for actual time worked, or a minimum of two (2) hours whichever is greater. The rate of compensation shall be in accordance with the Personnel Rules.

CALL BACK PAY (version 3)
Section 1. Employees starting a shift or called after the starting time of a shift shall receive not less than four (4) hours pay for the first period of shift; and, if required to continue on second period of shift, they shall receive pay for a full shift.
Section 2. Employees required to report for work not continuous with their regular assigned shift hours, or

on their normally scheduled days off, or holidays, shall receive not less than two (2) hours pay at double an employee's established hourly rate.

Section 3. Employees required to report for work and not used shall receive four (4) hours straight time pay.

Section 4. Voluntary Quit/Lay Off. Employees who voluntarily quit, voluntarily lay off, or are discharged for cause shall be paid only for actual hours worked.

Section 5. Any employee required to return to work before the employee's next work shift, and such call being made after the employee has left the Employer's premises at the end of the employee's last shift, shall be paid for a minimum of two (2) hours at double the employee's established hourly rate. The foregoing does not preclude the Employer from scheduling overtime, provided such overtime is scheduled before the end of the employee's work shift.

Section 6. Pager Pay. Any employee, except a regular lead or assistant lead, requested to be available for a will-call or carry a signal device home, shall be paid one (1) hour at double the employee's established hourly rate for the calendar day of availability.

Section 7. Emergency Callback. If an employee works less than two (2) hours minimum on an emergency callback during ice and snow conditions, overtime will commence at the time the employee leaves home.

Out of Title Work

Many contracts also deal with situations where an employer asks an employee to temporarily perform work in a different, normally higher pay grade, classification. This is sometimes referred to as "bumping" or "pushing up" into another position.

At issue in these clauses are the following:

- ❑ The "show must go on" – the company needs the flexibility to keep the work flowing even when employees are absent; the easiest way to accomplish this is by plugging in a current employee who is cross-trained to perform the position of the missing worker
- ❑ The company may not want to pay a premium to an employee who is learning a higher skilled position or who is only doing the work on a temporary or "fill-in" basis
- ❑ The employee wants to get paid the rate for the work he or she is actually doing
- ❑ The union wants to make sure that an employer does not have an incentive to rely on lower paid employees to perform higher-classification work

Out of title work clauses balance these concerns and ensure that there is a clear process to follow when employees perform out of classification jobs.

Clause Summaries and Drafting Notes

There is one sample clause below. It states that an employee performing in such a position will, under certain conditions, receive the higher rate of pay. The key provision is that the employee must perform at the higher rate for a significant period of time (22 days during any 6-month period) to qualify for the higher rate of pay. This is a favorable clause for management, since it only applies in situations where the job is performed for a significant period of time. The language would be very difficult to administer in a situation where an employee performs the higher level duties for more than 22 days and then alternates between the high and low classification – the clause does not specifically state how that situation might be handled.

This is not a typical provision. It is more common that the employee is paid starting with the first hour that they work in the higher classification and only paid during the time that they work in that classification. Other contracts state that an employee will be paid at the higher rate for all hours worked during a pay period when a certain number of hours in that pay period are worked at the higher classification. These latter two provisions are obviously less advantageous to the company who could end up paying a high rate of pay for hours that are performed at the lower rated classification.

In addition, the sample clause below has a provision that makes the supervisor liable if they misclassify an employee during a payroll period. This is also uncommon. This provision also states that the employee will return to their regular rate of pay when they go back to their regular job.

OUT OF TITLE WORK (version 1)
Section 1. Each time an employee is designated in writing by the employee's immediate supervisor to act in an established position in a higher classification than

the employee's permanent classification, and actually performs a major portion of the duties of the higher level position for a period of time more than twenty-two (22) workdays within any six (6) consecutive months, the employee shall be eligible to receive a promotional pay increase beginning with the 23rd day.

Section 2. If an employee's immediate supervisor who is covered by this Agreement inappropriately designates an employee to act in a vacant position in a higher classification, that supervisor may be held personally liable for reimbursing the Company for any promotional pay increase which results from the inappropriate assignment.

Section 3. Employees being paid at a higher rate while temporarily filling a position in a higher classification will be returned to their regular rate of pay when the period of temporary employment in the higher class is ended.

Disabilities Act
The Americans with Disabilities Act can significantly complicate the lives of both companies and unions. The act itself is difficult to understand and to implement. It provides that employers must reasonably accommodate qualified individuals with a disability. The regulations implementing the Act and subsequent court decisions state that the employer's responsibility to accommodate may include altering or waiving provisions of a collective bargaining agreement.

However, employers are not <u>always</u> required to waive collective bargaining agreement provisions. Thus the rights of qualified disabled employees are balanced against non-disabled employees with rights under the collective bargaining agreement. The interest of the employer, therefore, is to preserve its flexibility to accommodate disabled employees; the union wants to make sure that the labor agreement cannot be altered except in extreme circumstances.

Clause Summaries and Drafting Notes
The provision below gives the employer complete leeway to make the reasonable accommodation determination. It states that the company is allowed to waive contract provisions to accommodate an employee with a disability under the Americans with Disabilities Act. It does not provide for an appeal process for the union, nor does it require the company to negotiate with the union over the changes in the collective bargaining agreement. This is obviously a very favorable provision for the company; most unions are unlikely to give up their right to bargain over these

changes. On the other hand, the clause is ambiguous about the right of the union to object or grieve about accommodations that result in changes to the contract—this may leave the clause open to challenge.

AMERICANS WITH DISABILITIES ACT
Due to the Americans with Disabilities Act and the regulations promulgated thereunder, the Company may be required to make a reasonable accommodation to the disability of an applicant or incumbent employee that may be in conflict with provisions of this Agreement. In such event, the Company shall be privileged to make such accommodation notwithstanding the requirements of this Agreement. The Company shall notify the Union thereafter as soon as is practicable of such situation on a confidential basis.

Benefits

Benefits language in labor contracts is increasingly important, sometimes a strike issue. There are a number of different ways to deal with company benefits. There are three common formulations for providing benefits to employees under a union contract:

- ❑ The company pays employees a cash amount in lieu of benefits (this practice is common in the construction industry)
- ❑ The company pays the union an agreed upon amount per hour (or per month) to provide union sponsored benefit plans, administered by trustees of the union
- ❑ The company sponsors benefit plans (sometimes the same as those offered to nonunion workers, sometimes unique to the union members) and pays all or a portion of the premiums for those benefits.

There are several key concerns for employers and unions when reaching a compromise on benefits language:

- ❑ Who pays for benefits? Today the most important compromise is the basic cost of benefits, particularly health insurance costs which are skyrocketing
- ❑ Do employees share responsibility for benefits costs? Most negotiations today focus primarily on how increasing costs will be shared (if at all) between the company and union members – employer attempts to push a portion of benefit cost responsibility to employees has been a strike issue on several occasions recently; this

may be sharing premium expense, requiring co-pays or co-insurance, restrictions on prescription drug choices, and sometimes even language requiring employees to cover additional increases in premium during the term of the agreement

❑ What is covered? Because of the increased costs mentioned above, employer sponsors of the benefits plans may ask for language giving them authority to cancel or reduce benefits in order to reduce insurance costs

❑ Who manages the plan? Unions sometimes want employees in their own plans (this gives them more control over premiums paid and gives them access to the funds in the plan); other times they want employees in employer sponsored plans – companies are sometimes indifferent so long as employees receive coverage at a reasonable rate and their liability is limited; however, as benefit plans become under-funded, employers often want to avoid paying into union-sponsored plans

❑ Is there flexibility to deal with changes during the contract term? Companies usually want language that protects their ability to deal with changes during the term of the contract, or to alter plans without re-negotiating with the union.

Clause Summaries and Drafting Notes
Below are three examples of benefits clauses from various contracts that explore this range of solutions to the benefits issue. The first version simply lists the plans that the company provides. There is no

discussion of how much money the company will pay for these plans or how much the employee contribution will be for the plans (which presumably is negotiated as part of the pay package). Further the provision provides that the company can amend the plans and change them at any time and such changes are not subject to the grievance procedure in the contract. This language is strong for management.

The second version has a similar provision that simply lists the plan, saying that they are subject to the company plan documents. This version is more favorable to the union, however, because it gives the union the right to object to benefits issues under the grievance procedure in the contract. Additionally, the clause does not state under what conditions the company may change the plans in effect. Finally, there is a provision that work on a holiday will be subject to two and a half times the regular hourly rate (this is a bit of a strange place for this language – but that's what was negotiated in this agreement).

The third version is an extensive benefits plan outlining a number of different benefits including:
- Sick leave pay accumulated at a rate of one day per month and various provisions related to taking sick pay;
- An early retirement provision;
- Injury leave; bereavement leave; family medical leave;
- Life insurance; accidental death and dismemberment insurance

In addition this provision provides for medical

insurance, dental insurance and has various provisions regarding those benefits. The clause is somewhat favorable to the employer, simply listing that the employer is required to provide a certain number of plans without providing any specifics on those plans.

The employer is however required to provide specific types of coverage (PPO and HMO) and is prohibited from charging over certain amounts for employee premiums. These sections provide interesting examples of compromises designed to deal with the rapid rise in health insurance costs. Employees can only be required to pay $30 per month plus 25% of any total premium increases during the term of the contract, with the further provision that the employee contribution can never rise above 8 per cent of the total premium. These types of compromises are increasingly common in bargaining agreements. Finally, there is re-opener language in the provision as well.

BENEFITS (version 1)

All employees covered by this Agreement shall be subject to the provisions of and will be entitled to participation in the following of the Company's group benefit plan: [List Company Benefit Plans] as said plans are presently constituted or as said plans may be amended by the Company from time to time. The parties understand and agree that in the event such amendments take place during the term of this collective bargaining agreement, said amendments will apply automatically to covered employees.

It is further agreed that disputes under these plans will not be subject to the Grievance Procedure but will be governed solely by the terms of the benefit plan documents.

BENEFITS (version 2)

Section 1. Employee benefits shall be granted in accordance with Company Benefit Plan Documents. The implementation of the benefits shall be subject to the grievance procedure.

Section 2. Employees required to work on Company designated holidays will receive the regular rate of pay for the holiday (8 hours). Additionally, the employees will receive one and one-half (1.5) times the regular rate of pay for all hours worked. Employees' regular working schedules will determine holiday employment.

BENEFITS (version 3)

Section 1. Sick Leave. Employees shall accumulate sick leave at the rate of one (1) day per month with no limitation to the accumulation.

Section 2. Sick Leave: Notification, First Workday Missed. When an employee is unable to work because of illness, the employee shall notify the immediate supervisor, or designee, of the employee's absence and the reason therefore as promptly as available means of communication permits. Sick leave benefits will commence on the 2nd consecutive workday missed because of illness or injury, or the first workday missed in the case of hospitalization or incapacitating personal injury substantiated by a physician's certificate. The one-day waiting period must be satisfied as a precondition to sick leave benefits in each instance of absence due to illness or injury. A physician's certificate will not be automatically required as a precondition of sick leave benefits. However, the employer reserves the right to require a physician's certificate in the case of an extended illness; or, when the employer has evidence that an employee is abusing sick leave benefits, future absences may require a physician's certificate as a precondition to sick leave benefits.

Section 3. Dental Appointments. An employee shall be permitted time off for dental appointments. Time off for dental appointments will be charged to the employee's accumulated sick leave. The employee shall be required to furnish to the Employer a dentist's certificate of actual time off for such appointment. Appointments for dental work will be scheduled early or late in the day to keep interference with the employee's regular duties at a minimum.

Section 4. Sick Leave Pay Off. Upon retirement or termination, employees will be paid five percent (5%) of accumulated sick leave per year of service up to a maximum of fifty percent (50%) of 1,040 hours.

Section 5. Early Retirement. The Company will make fifty percent (50%) of unused sick leave as a retirement credit available to the employee. Any employee retiring may receive an early retirement benefit of continuation of medical insurance to age sixty-five (65) if the employee retires anytime after reaching the age of sixty-two (62) and has fifteen (15) or more years of service with the Employer.

Section 6. Injury Leave. Any employee who, during the life of this Agreement, sustains an injury which is accepted under the Workers Compensation laws shall, in addition to monies paid as statutory workers compensation benefits, receive from the

Employer an amount through the regular payroll system that combined with the monies paid as statutory benefits, will closely equal the employee's net straight time rate. Upon claim acceptance, an employee will not be required to use personal sick leave for a period not to exceed ninety (90) calendar days from the date upon which such Workers Compensation payments commence. The Employer may act to grant an additional sixty (60) calendar days coverage for a continuous period of disability. After any extension, the Employer may review the case for any further action it may wish to take. If no extension is granted after the ninety (90) day period, any future lost time paid through the payroll system, if authorized by the employee, may be charged against the employee's accumulated sick leave amount.

Section 7. Bereavement Leave. An employee shall be allowed three (3) days, but no more than 24 hours, time off duty without loss of pay by reason of the death of a member of the employee's immediate family. Immediate family is defined as spouse, parents, children, sister, brother, grandparent, grandchildren, mother-in-law, or father-in-law. Such time off shall be charged against Employer paid bereavement leave. An additional two (2) days, but no more than 16 hours, leave shall be allowed an employee if the employee must travel more than 150 miles one way to assist in making arrangements and/or to attend a funeral or services in the event of a death in the employee's immediate family. Approval for such travel time shall be made by the Maintenance Operations Manager or designee. Any additional time off shall also be granted only by the Maintenance Operations Manager or designee.

Section 8. Family Medical Leave. Eligible employees shall be entitled to leave as provided under and in compliance with federal and state family and medical leave laws. While on family medical leave, the employee may use accrued sick, vacation, and personal leave time to receive pay. Benefit entitlements accrue for those periods of time the employee remains in a pay status. When the pay status ends, medical, dental, and vision coverage may be continued on a self-pay basis.

Section 9. Medical and Vision. Any employee working eighty (80) hours or more in a calendar month is eligible for medical and vision benefits for the following month.

- ❑ **Medical Insurance:** The Employer will provide a choice of two (2) insurance carriers for employees and their eligible dependents; one carrier will be for a comprehensive major medical plan, the second will be a plan provided by a health maintenance organization. In the event the insurance carrier is changed, the coverage will be equal to or better than the present coverage.

- ❑ **Vision Insurance:** The Employer will provide a vision care program for employees and their eligible dependents that covers basic vision service.

Section 10. Dental Insurance. Dental insurance for employees and their eligible dependents is effective on the first of the month after three (3) full calendar months of employment, provided at least eighty (80) hours are worked in each month. Following initial eligibility, employees continuing to work at least eighty (80) hours in a calendar month will be eligible for dental benefits for themselves and their eligible dependents for the following month. There will be a choice of two carriers, one of which will be the [Union Dental Program]. If the Employer switches from [Current Dental Coverage], the Employer will offer a plan of equal or better coverage. Any change in carriers will be effective the following January 1.

Section 11. Extended Absences: Self-pay Premiums. Employees who are laid off, or are on an extended sick leave absence and not in a pay status, shall be allowed to self-pay medical insurance premiums in accord with federal and state law.

Section 12. Life Insurance. A Twenty Thousand Dollar ($20,000) life insurance policy will be provided each employee. Effective January 1, 2001, a Forty Thousand Dollar ($40,000) life insurance policy will be provided each employee.

Section 13. AD&D Insurance. One Hundred Thousand Dollars ($100,000) Accidental Death and Dismemberment insurance coverage will be provided each employee.

Section 14. Premium Maximums. Effective the first of the month following Commission approval, employees will pay by payroll deduction a monthly contribution of thirty dollars ($30.00) for medical, dental and vision insurance. Effective January 1, 2002, in addition to this monthly contribution, employees will pay 25% of any premium increases over the January 2001 premium. At no time will the employee's cumulative share of the premium cost exceed 8% of the total blended monthly composite premium. The Union may open negotiations solely on the issue of Health and Welfare during 2001 and 2002 by giving the Employer a minimum of thirty (30) days notice. If no agreement is reached by the parties, Health and Welfare will stay the same as it was prior to the start of these negotiations.

Probationary Period

Most companies and unions include in their collective bargaining agreements a probationary period for new employees. This probation is provided for a number of reasons. First, it gives the employer an opportunity to determine whether or not the employee is going to work out over the long term. Second, it gives the employee an opportunity to see if they are going to stay in the job. Third, it avoids the administrative hassle, for both the employer and the union, from getting the person on (and off) the rolls for paying union dues if they are ultimately not going to work out. Finally, it prevents the grievance and arbitration framework from being filled up by complaints from employees with almost no seniority, who the company and the union have little vested interest in keeping around.

These provisions typically deal with two issues. First, that the employee does not have the right to avail themselves of the grievance and arbitration procedures and that the employer does not have to have "just cause" to terminate their employment. Second, the employee is not considered a union member or fee payer, and is not subject to the payment of union dues or fees.

Clause Summaries and Drafting Notes

There are two model probationary clauses included below. The first version provides for a 6-month probationary period and states that any absences will extend the probationary period by the length of the absences. It states that there is no just cause requirement for the termination of the employee and the employee is not allowed to avail himself of the grievance procedure. This is a relatively long probation period (most are about half that length, or 90 days) and the clause is a favorable one for management.

The second version uses the more common 90-day probationary period. It also provides that the employer does not have to prove a termination of a probationary employee is for "just cause" and that a probationary employee is not entitled to use the grievance procedure.

PROBATIONARY PERIOD (version 1)
Section 1. Each new or rehired employee shall be on probation for the first six (6) months of employment or reemployment in the bargaining unit. Upon satisfactory completion of said probationary period, seniority will be computed from the date of hire, or most recent date of rehire, with the Company.
Section 2. Absence from work will extend the probationary period for a period of time equivalent to the length of such absence.
Section 3. At any time during the probationary period, an employee may be discharged for any reason. Such employee so discharged shall not have any recourse under this Agreement, including the right to file a grievance.

PROBATIONARY PERIOD (version 2)
A period of ninety (90) working days for persons newly employed by the Employer shall constitute an introductory period during which the Employer shall have the right to discharge without any limitations by the Union or this Agreement.

Seniority

The seniority clause is one of the most important for unions after the union security and dues check off clauses. The vast majority of labor agreements deal in some fashion with the issue of seniority. Historically, unions have demanded seniority be the key in determining wage levels, promotions or layoff decisions. Employers, on the other hand, typically want seniority only to be one factor among many that will determine promotions or layoffs.

The core interests at stake in these clauses are both philosophical as well as practical. Philosophically, the issue at stake in the seniority compromise is the balance between rewarding longevity and rewarding performance. Unions normally want to reward longevity because it is completely objective and "fair" to members. Seniority was considered a proxy (albeit a somewhat ham-handed one) for skill, productivity and experience. It is a way to reward loyalty to the company and the union. In a time where lifetime employment was the model and factory production was less complex than today, this philosophy made some sense.

As the economy became more competitive and production became more complex, employers increasingly wanted to shift rewards away from seniority. Employers sought to reward employees who were most skilled, whether senior or not, over those with low skills but long tenure. Employers over the last decade or so have increasingly won this argument at the bargaining table. Nevertheless, seniority still plays a much more prominent role in the work conditions of unionized operations than non-union ones.

Beyond the philosophy of how much to rely on seniority, there is the mechanics of the seniority compromise that is an important part of these clauses. The clause must identify:

- ❑ Where seniority will play a role (promotions, wage rates, layoff, vacations, etc.)
- ❑ What counts as seniority (time in the current job, time in the current department, time in the organization as a whole, etc.)
- ❑ What events "break" the employee's seniority, and under what conditions can an employee receive credit for prior service
- ❑ How seniority controls in the job decisions (is it the controlling factor, one factor among many, or solely a tiebreaker)
- ❑ Are some employees granted special seniority status (union trustees or stewards are sometimes awarded "super-seniority")?

Clause Summaries and Drafting Notes
Since the seniority compromise is so prevalent in collective bargaining agreements there are seven different versions of seniority clauses included here. Each one is slightly different from the others although many share common compromises that are often made between companies and unions on the seniority issue.

The first version defines seniority as length of service with the company. Seniority is defined as only one factor in determining layoff or promotion along with ability, skill, and performance. This is a very favorable clause for management and allows decisions to be made without strict reliance on seniority. The clause also outlines conditions that can lead to a loss of seniority.

The second version also defines seniority as length of service with the company and identifies that it affects the employee's right to layoffs or rehire. The clause states that layoff is by occupation only, but length of service in the plant controls over length of service in the occupation. This is favorable to the union, especially to longer-term members of the union, and less favorable to the company who in some circumstances could be forced to layoff an employee with significant experience in a particular job over a more "senior" employee with little experience in that classification. The clause also gives employees the right to transfer into other occupations so long as the employee is qualified and has higher seniority. This is a favorable clause for the union.

The third version may seem confusing at first, since it outlines only conditions for a break in seniority but does not provide further clarification as to how seniority is used. Read alone this seniority clause does not seem to protect employee rights at all. However, this clause should be read in conjunction with other clauses in the agreement (like layoff or promotion clauses) that state where and how seniority will control. It is included to give the reader notice that sometimes the seniority compromise is included elsewhere in the agreement; further, it provides a good list of common reasons for breaks in service.

The fourth version is an example of the traditional

seniority clauses in older union agreements. It states clearly that layoffs are strictly by company seniority and that other factors like performance or skill play no role in the layoff decision. Most organizations attempt to achieve a compromise on this issue, but this is the classic seniority provision.

The fifth version is like version four in that seniority is the controlling factor, although it does provide a qualifier that states that the most senior employee will not be able to bump others if that employee is not able to perform the work. This is a limited exception, but it does at least give the employer an argument to prevent seniority from controlling in every circumstance.

The sixth version is a much more pro-management clause, stating that seniority is only one factor along with other qualifications. This clause clearly states that seniority only acts as a tiebreaker in situations where all other factors combined are equal.

Finally, the seventh version is an example of a "super seniority" clause. This is a clause that provides additional union security for, in this case, trustees, union officers, shop stewards, and executive board members. There are two reasons for a provision like this. First, it insures that the employees that remain after a layoff will have union leadership in place. It prevents the union leadership from being decimated by a layoff decision. Second, such a provision acts as a reward or perk for union officers and other activists.

SENIORITY (version 1)
Section 1. Seniority for the purposes of this

Agreement is defined as the length of continuous service with the Company.

Section 2. In assigning employees to higher-paying jobs, or in the case of layoff due to lack of work, the Company shall select those employees who are best qualified to be so promoted or retained. In making such selections, consideration will be given to such factors as ability, performance, skill and the principle of seniority. Judgments as to qualifications shall be at the sole discretion of the Company.

Section 3. Employees shall lose all seniority rights and employment shall cease for any of the following reasons:

a. Resignation
b. Discharge
c. Failure to report to work within three (3) days after recall from layoff
d. Absence due to layoff for 120 days
e. If the employee overstays a leave of absence
f. If the employee gives a false reason for a leave of absence, or engages in other employment during such leave
g. If any monetary settlement is made with the employee covering total disability
h. If the employee is retired
i. If the employee falsifies information on his application for employment. The falsity may come to light at any time after the employee's date of hire of acquiring seniority.
j. If the employee is absent from work for non-industrial illness or injury in excess of three (3) calendar months or for industrial illness or injury in excess of six (6) calendar months
k. Failure to report for a period of three (3) days

SENIORITY (version 2)

Seniority shall be based upon length of service from the date of hiring in the plant. In all cases of layoffs, rehiring and transfers, length of service within the plant shall govern within each of the occupations listed in Schedule A attached hereto. In the event a layoff is required, then the employee in that occupation who has the shortest seniority in the plant, rather than in that occupation, shall be the first to be laid off. Rehiring within any occupation shall be in the reverse order to that in which the employees were laid off.

So far as is reasonably practical, the Employer will transfer employees (by virtue of their plant-wide seniority and who would otherwise be laid off) to work in another group or department, provided that they are qualified and competent to do the job to which they are transferred. An employee accepting another job in lieu of layoff shall be entitled to the job from which he was laid off when it becomes active.

SENIORITY (version 3)

The length of continuous service of an employee shall be deemed broken for any of the following reasons:
1. If the employee voluntarily terminates employment.
2. If the employee is discharged.
3. If the employee, within ninety-six (96) hours after date of mailing notice of recall by registered mail, does not notify the Employer that he will return to work immediately.
4. If the employee is absent for forty-eight (48) or more consecutive hours without excuse.

5. If the employee has not been reemployed by the Employer within twelve (12) months from the date of the employee's last layoff.

SENIORITY (version 4)
Seniority shall govern or determine layoffs and recalls, promotions and transfers. Increases or decreases in the work force shall be by seniority. Layoffs and recalls after layoffs shall be in order of seniority, i.e., the last hired shall be the first laid off and recalls shall be in reverse order.

SENIORITY (version 5)
In layoffs and recalls seniority shall control, provided the senior employee has the ability to do the available work. In promotions, seniority shall govern, if the employee has the capability, physical fitness and experience for the job.

SENIORITY (version 6)
Seniority shall consist of (or be governed by) the following factors:
1. Length of service
2. Qualifications, ability, skill, experience, physical fitness, and job performance

If, as between two or more employees, their qualifications, ability, job performance, experience, and physical fitness are relatively equal, then length of service shall govern.

SUPERSENIORITY (version 7)
Seniority lay-offs and recalls shall be by categories, departments and operations, not plant-wide, both as to

existing and new departments and operations.

In any event, the Union trustees, sergeants at arms, Shop Stewards and Executive Board, not exceeding respectively three (3), two (2), three (3) and nine (9) in number, the President, Vice-President, Financial Secretary and Recording Secretary of the Union, shall, during their respective terms of office, have plant-wide seniority on lay-offs and recalls, provided such official can satisfactorily perform the operation affected.

Job Posting/Transfer/Promotion

Clauses covering job postings, transfers, promotions and other job changes are normally considered seniority compromises. These clauses deal with how job promotions, transfers within departments, and similar changes will be dealt with in the organization. Sometimes these areas are simply considered part of the management rights compromise and not a part of the bargaining agreement.

At its core, a job posting program essentially insures that promotions and transfers are handled out in the open, subject to scrutiny by the union and its members. Usually an organization will give notification to the union as well as to bargaining unit members regarding any job positions that become available and will post these positions for a reasonable period of time. This gives all employees that wish to be considered for the opportunity a chance to apply.

The key interests that help define the job posting, transfer or promotion compromise include the following:

- ❑ Management's interest in making job changes, promotions or transfers quickly and without undue interference
- ❑ The union's interest in having a say in how these changes are made (i.e. ensuring they are made based on objective factors and not based on discriminatory factors or favoritism)
- ❑ The union's interest in protecting and rewarding the loyalty of long-time union members and ensuring that these changes are not made in a way that discriminates against older or more

active union members

Clause Summaries and Drafting Notes

Like with the seniority compromises discussed earlier, unions typically want such decisions to be made based on seniority alone while companies instead would prefer to have decisions based on performance related factors. The key details that are normally defined in these clauses include:

- ❏ Whether there is a requirement to post or otherwise notify employees of job openings
- ❏ The length of time a position must be posted, where it must be posted
- ❏ The factors management may include in deciding who wins a job bid
- ❏ The circumstances under which management may ignore or not follow the procedure (temporary transfers, no qualified applicants, etc.)

There are five model clauses included below. The first is a typical job posting policy, and it is relatively favorable to management. It states that it allows bids on jobs and that the company will use seniority, job requirements, skill, and fitness for duty all as factors in deciding whether or not an employee will receive a job position. It states that seniority will be considered a tiebreaker among equally qualified candidates.

The second version is limited only to job transfers. It clarifies that seniority is determined based on the classification you are transferring from. It also states that transfers will be for 30 days only and must be with the consent of the union and employee. This clause is somewhat favorable to the union, relying heavily on seniority and prohibiting long-term transfers without a permanent change in status by the company.

The third version is another job transfer provision which states that employees must request reassignment and that their request lasts for one year. Employees are given an opportunity to reassign based on company needs. The company also has the right to use an involuntary reassignment where circumstances require it. Seniority is a factor in all transfer requests, but the company is allowed to transfer a less senior employee where it feels that this individual is best qualified. In these cases all higher seniority employees are informed of the decision to transfer the less senior employee and they have the right to grieve that decision.

The fourth clause outlines a promotion policy. It relies heavily on company-wide seniority, although any employee applying must also meet the job requirements for the position coming available. It also provides that any promotion decision is on a trial basis and the employee is allowed to return to their old job if they are unable to perform the new position. This clause is a pretty good compromise between the company's interest in making sure the employee is capable of performing the job and the union's interest in protecting seniority. Of course the key issue is how the company proves whether the employee can adequately perform the job, which ultimately will decide grievances over the application of the clause. This is not clear in the clause. If the company wanted to improve its chances in front of an arbitrator it might choose to include some statement about the criteria it is allowed to use when judging suitability in the position or, better yet, a statement that the company's decisions regarding suitability are not subject to the grievance procedure.

The fifth version is also a promotion policy. It states that employees must fill out a request for promotion form that expires annually. Management is required to notify employees if the position for which they have applied has been filled. This clause defines a probationary period for all promotion decisions and provides that decisions made under this clause are grievable. Finally, it specifically provides that promotion decisions that are made outside of this clause be rescinded where the policy is not followed. This clause is relatively strong for the union, although it does leave open the criteria management may use in making promotion decisions. Although this is not always in management's favor (the union can always grieve the criteria used) many arbitrators will leave the decision up to management if there is no clear limit provided in the contract.

JOB POSTING (version 1)
All employee vacancies and new jobs created shall be posted for five (5) days to allow employees to make application in writing for such jobs. The company will give careful consideration to applications received in relation to the following qualifications: (a) seniority, (b) requirements of the job, (c) individual skill, efficient service and physical fitness. Where qualifications (b) and (c) are relatively the same, seniority shall govern.

JOB TRANSFER (version 2)

An employee who is temporarily transferred from his regular job classification to another job classification shall continue to accrue seniority in his regular job classification. The Company shall notify the Union whenever an employee has been temporarily transferred for a period of thirty (30) consecutive calendar days. The period of a temporary transfer shall not exceed thirty (30) days without the consent of the employee and the Union. Seniority shall prevail in all transfers so far as practicable.

JOB TRANSFER (version 3)

Employees who have attained permanent status and who meet all eligibility requirements shall have the opportunity to request reassignment to vacant positions within their respective agencies in accordance with the provisions of this Article.

Section 1. Definitions.

(A)   "Duty station" shall mean the place, which is designated as an employee's official work area.

(B)   "Change in duty station" shall mean the moving of an employee to a duty station located outside of his current duty station.

(C)   "Occupational level" shall mean the same level within the employee's current occupation within the Company classification system.

(D)   "Reassignment" shall mean the moving of an employee from one position in a class/occupational level to a different position in the same class/occupational level with the same essential knowledge, skills and abilities, regardless of the location of the position.

(E)   "Transfer" shall mean the moving of an

employee from one work area of the Company to a different work area.

(F)   "Company needs" are those actions which the Company must take in order to meet its mission.

Section 2. Procedures.

(A)   An employee who has attained permanent status may apply for a reassignment on a Request for Reassignment Form (supplied by the Company). Such requests shall indicate work location(s) or shift(s) to which the employee would like to be reassigned.

(B)   An employee may submit a Request for Reassignment Form at any time; however, all such requests shall expire on May 31 of each calendar year. Requests can be filed in May to become effective on June 1.

(C)   All Request for Reassignment Forms shall be submitted to the Plant Manager or his designee who shall be responsible for furnishing a copy of each such request to the manager(s) or supervisor(s) who have the authority to make employee hiring decisions in the work unit to which the employee has requested reassignment.

(D)   Except where a vacancy is filled by demotion, the manager or supervisor having hiring authority for that vacancy shall give first consideration to those employees who have submitted a Request for Reassignment Form; provided, however, that employees whose request for reassignment is not submitted by the first day of the month shall not be considered for vacancies which occur during that month.

(E)   The hiring authority shall normally fill a permanent vacancy with the employee who has the greatest length of service in the class/occupational level and who has a Request for Reassignment Form on file for the vacancy. The parties agree, however, that other factors, such as employees' work history and Company needs, will be taken into consideration in making the decision as to whether or not the employee with the greatest length of service in the class/occupational level will be placed in the vacant position.

(F)   If the employee with the greatest length of service in the class/occupational level is not selected for the vacant position, all employees who have greater length of service in the class/occupational level than the employee selected shall be notified in writing of the Company's decision.

(G)   When an employee has been reassigned pursuant to a Request filed under this Article, all other pending Requests for Reassignment from that employee shall be canceled. No other Request for Reassignment may be filed by the employee under this Article for a period of twelve (12) months following the employee's reassignment. If an employee declines an offer of reassignment pursuant to a Request filed under this Article, the employee's Request shall be canceled and the employee will not be eligible to resubmit that Request for a period of twelve (12) months from the date the employee declined the offer of reassignment.

Section 3. Involuntary Reassignment, Transfer or Change in Duty Station. Nothing contained in this Agreement shall be construed to prevent the

Company, at its discretion, from effecting the involuntary reassignment, transfer or change in duty station of any employee according to the needs of the Company; however, the Company will make a good faith effort to take such action only when dictated by the needs of the Company and in each case, will take into consideration the needs and circumstances of the employee prior to taking such action.

Section 4. Notice. An employee shall be given a minimum of fourteen (14) calendar days notice prior to the Company effecting any reassignment or transfer of the employee. In the case of a transfer, the Company will make a good faith effort to give a minimum of thirty (30) calendar days notice. The parties agree, however, that these notice requirements shall not be required during an emergency or other extraordinary conditions.

Section 5. Grievability. The provisions of this Article shall not be subject to the grievance procedures of Article 6 of this Agreement; however, an employee complaint concerning improper application of the provisions of Paragraph (E) of Section 2 and Section 3 may be grieved in accordance with Article 6, up to and including Step 3 of the Grievance Procedure. In considering such complaints, weight shall be given to the specific procedures followed and decisions made, along with the needs of the Company.

PROMOTION (version 4)

Promotions shall be made on the basis of company-wide seniority provided the ability of the senior employee meets the job requirements. Employees promoted to a higher grade shall be on a trial basis of one (1) to four (4) weeks on the job after the date of promotion. If during the trial period, the employee is not able to satisfactorily perform the job as required, such employee shall be returned to the former job and former rate of pay.

PROMOTION (version 5)

The Company and the Union agree that promotions should be used to provide career mobility within the Company and should be based on the relative merit and fitness of applicants. Toward the goals of selecting the most qualified applicant for each promotional vacancy, the parties agree that the provisions of this Article, along with all provisions of the Personnel Rules, will be followed when making such appointments.

Section 1. Definitions. As used in this Article:

(A) "Occupational level" shall mean the same level within the employee's current occupation within the Company classification system.

(B) "Promotion" shall mean the moving of an employee from a position in one class/occupational level to a different position in another class/occupational level having a higher maximum salary.

(C) "Demotion" shall mean the moving of an employee from a position in one class/occupational level to a different position in another class/occupational level having a lower maximum salary.

Section 2. Procedures

(A) An employee who has attained permanent status in the Company may apply for a promotion by submitting a Request for Promotion Form, furnished by the Company in which the promotional position is located, to be considered for promotional vacancies. Such requests shall indicate the class(es)/occupational level(s) and/or other work locations to which the employee would like to be promoted.

(B)   An employee may submit a Request for Promotion at any time; however, all such requests shall expire on May 31 of each calendar year.

(C)   When an employee has been promoted pursuant to a Request filed under this Article, all other pending Requests for Promotion from that employee shall be canceled. No other Requests for Promotion may be filed by that employee under this Article for a period of twelve (12) months following the employee's promotion.

Section 3. Method of Filling Vacancies

(A)   Except where a vacancy is filled by demotion, or by reassignment as defined in Article 9 of this Agreement, those employees who have applied for promotion in accordance with Section 2 shall be given first consideration for promotional vacancies in accordance with the agencies' standard selection process.

(B)   Each employee who applies in accordance with Section 2 will be notified in writing by the appointing authority when the position has been filled.

Section 4. Probationary Status on Promotion

(A)   An employee who has been appointed to a classification or occupational level shall attain permanent status in that classification or occupational level upon successful completion of the designated probationary period. Such employee shall not lose permanent status in such classification or occupational level.

(B)   An employee who has obtained permanent status in a classification or occupational level who fails, due to performance, to satisfactorily complete the probation in the promotional classification or occupational level shall be demoted to the former classification or occupational level previously held by the employee in an available vacant position.

    i.   Such a demotion shall be with permanent status, provided the employee held permanent status in the lower class/occupational level.

    ii.   The employee's salary will be reduced in accordance with the Company's pay upon demotion policy.

    iii.   Such demotion shall not be grievable under the contractual grievance procedure.

    iv.   Such demotion shall not preclude the Company from seeking to discipline the employee for just cause based upon specific acts of misconduct.

Section 5. Grievability

(A)   The provisions of this Article may be grieved in accordance with Article 6, up to and including Step 3 of the Grievance Procedure whose decision shall be final and binding.

(B)   Should the Human Resources Director determine that the standard selection process was not followed in filling a promotional vacancy, they shall have the authority, among other remedies, to order that the promotion be rescinded and direct that the promotion be re-conducted in accordance with the standard selection process.

Layoff

Layoff provisions are another compromise on the seniority issue. They place conditions on when a company can decide to reconstitute its work complement. The key interests that help define the layoff compromise include the following:

- Management's interest in adjusting its workforce according to its business requirements quickly and without undue interference
- In any layoff situation, management typically wants to keep its most productive employees
- The union's interest in having a say in how these changes are made (i.e. ensuring they are made based on objective factors and not based on discriminatory factors or favoritism)
- The union's interest in protecting and rewarding the loyalty of long-time union members and ensuring that these changes are not made in a way that discriminates against older or more active union members

Clause Summaries and Drafting Notes

Unions often want layoff decisions to be made based on seniority alone while companies instead would prefer to have decisions based on performance related factors. The key details normally defined in these clauses include:

- Under what circumstances the company can call for a layoff (this is normally considered a decision left up to the company as part of the management rights compromise)
- When and how the union and its members are to be notified of any layoff decision
- The factors management can consider in making

the layoff decision (seniority, productivity, job skill, cross-training, active discipline, quality, safety, etc.)

❑ The rights of employees on layoff (unemployment, recall rights, bumping rights of other employees, etc.)

There are two model versions of layoff clauses provided. The first version states that layoffs will be based on seniority in the plant and <u>not</u> in the classification. It states that you can use seniority to keep a position in any classification as long as you have at least four months seniority within the classification. Finally, it gives the employee the ability to transfer to other work areas if they have more plant-wide seniority than employees who are designated to stay in those areas. This version is very favorable for the union, essentially protecting the most senior employees no matter their skill level in a particular classification.

Version two states that seniority is defined by classification within the bargaining unit. This means that plant seniority controls where seniority in the classification is longer than other employees in that classification. This provision also utilizes a retention points formula based on performance standards over the prior 5-year period. Seniority is only one of the factors considered and acts as a tiebreaker in those situations where overall qualifications are equal. The provision provides a 14-day notice provision for layoffs or a payment in lieu of notice. It also provides for demotion or reassignment in cases where an employee has seniority in other classifications. Finally, it also has a notice provision for the union and recall rights for employees laid off. This clause is pretty favorable for management in that it relies more on performance than seniority and gives the company the right to award the retention points.

LAYOFF (version 1)
Section 1. In the event of a permanent layoff that involves regular employees in a department, regular employees having least seniority will be laid off first provided that employees with greater seniority have ability, and provided the senior employee accepts the job.

Section 2. At time of layoff, employees may exercise seniority in any job classification provided they have a minimum of four (4) months seniority gained with the Company in the job classification and provided further that whenever the order of layoff is based on a greater period of seniority gained in the job classification, the employee shall have the minimum seniority gained in the job classification, as set forth in the Seniority Schedules, in order to exercise seniority over an employee who does have the minimum seniority in that job classification.

Section 3. Seniority shall be based upon length of service from the date of hiring in the plant. In all cases of layoffs, rehiring and transfers, length of service within the plant shall govern within each of the occupations listed in Schedule A attached hereto. In the event a layoff is required, then the employee in that occupation who has the shortest seniority in the plant, rather than in that occupation, shall be the first to be laid off. Rehiring within any occupation shall be in the reverse order to that which the employees were laid off.

Section 4. So far as is reasonably practical, the

Employer will transfer employees (by virtue of their plant-wide seniority and who would otherwise be laid off) to work in another group or department, provided that they are qualified and competent to do the job to which they are transferred. An employee accepting another job in lieu of layoff shall be entitled to the job from which he was laid off when it becomes active.

LAYOFF (version 2)
Section 1. Layoffs.
(A)   When unit employees are to be laid off, the Company shall implement such layoff in accordance with the following manner:
  a. Layoff shall be by classification within the bargaining unit.
  b. No employee with permanent status in the affected classification shall be laid off while an employee who does not hold permanent status is serving in that classification unless the permanent employee does not elect to exercise his retention rights or does not meet the selective competition criteria.
  c. All employees who have permanent status in the affected class or level shall be ranked on a layoff list based on the total retention points derived as follows:
    i. Length of service retention points shall be based on one point for each month of continuous service.
    ii. An employee who moves from one bargaining unit position to accept employment in another bargaining unit position is not considered to

have a break in service.

    iii. An employee who has been laid off and is reemployed within one year from the date of the layoff, shall not be considered to have a break in service.

  d. Moving from bargaining unit position to non-bargaining unit or management position and back to bargaining unit position does not constitute a break in service unless the employee's break in service is more than 31 calendar days. Only time spent in the bargaining unit can be counted in calculating retention points.

(B) Retention points deducted for not meeting performance standards or work expectations defined for the position shall be based on the five years immediately prior to the company's established cutoff date. Five points shall be deducted for each month an employee has a rating below performance expectations.

  a. The layoff list shall be prepared by totaling retention points.

  b. The employee with the highest total retention points is placed at the top of the list, and the employee with the lowest retention points is placed at the bottom of the list.

  c. The employee at the top of the list shall bump the employee at the bottom of the list. The next highest employee on the list and the remaining employees shall be handled in the same manner until the total number of filled positions in the class to be abolished is complete.

d. Should two or more employees have the same combined total of retention points, the order of layoff shall be determined by giving preference for retention in the following sequence:

    i. The employee with the longest service in the affected classification.

    ii. The employee with the longest continuous service.

e. An employee who has permanent status and who is to be laid off shall be given at least 14 calendar days notice of such layoff or in lieu thereof, two weeks pay or a combination of days of notice and pay, in lieu of the full 14 calendar days notice, to be paid at the employee's current hourly base rate of pay. The notice of layoff shall be in writing and sent to the employee by certified mail, return receipt requested. Within 7 calendar days after receiving the notice of layoff, the employee shall have the right to request a demotion or reassignment in lieu of layoff to a position in a classification within the bargaining unit which the employee held permanent status, or to a position in a classification at the level of or below the classification in the bargaining unit, in which the employee held permanent status. Such request must be in writing and reassignment or demotion cannot be affected to a higher class within the series.

 f. An employee's request for demotion or reassignment shall be granted unless it would cause the layoff of another employee who possesses a greater total of retention points.

 g. An employee who is adversely affected as a result of another employee having a greater number of retention points shall have the same right of reassignment or demotion under the same procedure as provided in this section.

 h. If an employee requests a demotion or reassignment in lieu of layoff, the same formula and criteria for establishing retention points for that class shall be used as prescribed in this section.

(C) If there is to be a layoff of employees, the Company shall take all reasonable steps to place any adversely affected employees in existing vacancies for which they are qualified.

(D) If work performed by employees in this unit is to be performed by non-Company employees, the Company agrees to encourage the employing entity to consider any adversely affected unit employees for employment in its organization if the Company has been unable to place the employees in other positions within the Company.

Section 2. Job Security. The Company shall make a reasonable effort to notify the Union at least thirty (30) days in advance of classifications within the bargaining unit that will be involved in a layoff. Prior to the actual layoff, or scheduled closing, the Company will meet with the Union to discuss the effect of the layoff on the employees involved.

Section 3. Recall. When a vacancy occurs, or new position is established, laid off employees shall be recalled in the following manner:

(A)   For one year following layoff, when a position is to be filled, the laid off employees with the highest number of retention points shall be offered reemployment and subsequent offers shall be made in the order of the employee's total retention points. Reemployment of such employees shall be with permanent status. An employee who refuses such offer of reemployment shall forfeit any rights to subsequent placement offers as provided in this subsection.

(B)   An employee who accepts a voluntary demotion in lieu of layoff and is subsequently promoted to a position in the same classification from which the employee was demoted in lieu of layoff, shall be promoted with permanent status.

(C)   Under no circumstances is a layoff to be considered as a disciplinary action, and in the event an employee elects to appeal the action taken, such appeal must be based upon whether the layoff was in accordance with the provisions of this Article.

Holidays

Many companies provide for holiday benefits as part of the benefits of working for the organization.

Companies will typically list in their labor contracts the holidays that are included. In addition, they will provide some rules for dealing with cases where employees are required to work on the designated holiday or conditions in which holiday pay is not available to employees. The basic interests at issue in these clauses are:

- ❏ Whether or not the company will compensate additional amounts for work on holidays
- ❏ The company's right to schedule work on holidays
- ❏ The union's interest in making sure that its members are either able to be with their families on holidays or, if required to work, are compensated for holiday work

Clause Summaries and Drafting Notes

There are three holiday clauses included below. The basic issues debated when working on these clauses are:

- ❏ Which holidays, if any, are recognized in the contract
- ❏ How employees not required to work on the holiday are compensated for that holiday (if at all)
- ❏ How employees required to work on the holiday are compensated
- ❏ How the company will decide who works on designated holidays, including any notification procedure
- ❏ Penalties for employees who fail or refuse to

perform work on a holiday shift when assigned to do so

The first model clause is a typical holiday policy. It lists the holidays and establishes a handful of requirements for being paid for the holidays. It requires that the employee be past his probationary period and not on layoff status or leave of absence. It also requires that the employee work the day before and the day after the holiday in order to be paid. Finally, it extends a vacation by any holidays that fall within the designated vacation. This is the typical compromise.

The second version, after listing the holidays, also provides that an employee must be employed for at least 60 days continuously before the holiday in order to qualify for holiday pay. It has a similar requirement to work before and after the holiday.

The third version lists the holidays and provides holiday pay at two times the normal hourly rate. It also provides for personal days, stating that employees can take personal days after 6 months of employment with a 30-day notice that the employee intends to take the day. There is a similar requirement that the employee work the day before and after in order to receive the holiday pay and if required to work on that day the employee receives his regular rate of pay for hours worked plus the two times pay for the holiday. Finally, it states that an employee must work 30 days before becoming eligible for holiday pay and must be on "pay" status unless on an approved or temporary absence. This is a very favorable holiday clause for the union and its members.

HOLIDAYS (version 1)

Section 1. The following holidays shall be observed: [List Holidays].

Section 2. To be eligible to receive holiday pay, an employee:

(A)   Must be past his probationary period, and

(B)   Must not be on a leave of absence or on layoff; and

(C)   Must have worked the scheduled day before and the scheduled day after the holiday unless said absence is excused by management.

Section 3. If any of the aforesaid holidays falls during the employee's vacation period, the employee will be allowed one extra day of vacation with pay.

HOLIDAYS (version 2)

Section 1. The following days will be considered holidays for the purpose of this article: [List Holidays].

Section 2. In order to qualify for holiday pay under this section, an employee must meet all of the following conditions:

(A)   The employee shall have sixty (60) days or more of continuous service with the Company immediately prior to the holiday.

(B)   The employee performs his scheduled hours of work on his last scheduled work day preceding the holiday and also on his first scheduled work day following the holiday.

Employees scheduled to work on a holiday but failing to report for and perform such work shall not be entitled to any holiday pay.

HOLIDAYS (version 3)

Section 1. Holidays shall be recognized as follows and paid for two (2) times the straight time hourly rate: New Year's Day, President's Day, Memorial Day, Independence Day, Labor Day, Thanksgiving Day, the day after Thanksgiving Day and Christmas Day. In addition, on thirty (30) days notice, each employee shall have the right (after six (6) months employment) to select three (3) personal leave days of the employee's choice each fiscal year. The three (3) personal leave days may not be carried over from year to year.

Section 2. If one of the holidays referred to in Section 1 above falls on the employee's first consecutive day off, the preceding work day will be observed as the holiday. If the holiday falls on the employee's second consecutive day off, the following work day will be observed as the holiday, except employees working a 10-hour shift schedule may choose to take the preceding work day off with the approval of the supervisor. If the holiday falls on the employee's third consecutive day off, the following work day will be observed as the holiday.

Section 3. The Employer also retains the right to require the employee to work on a recognized holiday, in which case the employee shall be compensated in accordance with this contract and in addition shall receive holiday pay as defined in Section 2.

Section 4. Employees working a ten (10) hour day, four (4) day work week may elect to utilize two (2) hour vacation leave to receive a full ten (10) hours holiday pay.

Section 5. In order to qualify for holiday pay, the employee must:
have been in the employ of the Employer for thirty (30) days; and

work on both the regularly scheduled work day prior to and the regularly scheduled work day following the applicable holiday; and

be on pay status on the work day prior to or the work day following such holiday, or where such an absence was approved by the Employer or a temporary layoff not to exceed fifteen (15) calendar days.

Hours of Work/Overtime

These provisions are also very common in labor contracts. They normally state the basic work rules regarding when employees are required to show up for work and how schedules will be dealt with by the employer. The main interests at issue in bargaining these clauses are:

- ❏ Management's right to set the basic working conditions and work schedules for employees
- ❏ Management's interest in adjusting and changing the regular working schedule based on work requirements
- ❏ Management's interest in being able to schedule overtime hours when needed
- ❏ Management's interest in not incurring significant overtime premium pay when overtime is necessary
- ❏ The union's interest in making sure members are able to plan around a regular working schedule, including if possible, a guaranteed number of hours of work per week
- ❏ The union's interest in work schedules that cannot be changed unreasonably (if at all) without consulting the union
- ❏ The union's interest in making sure members are fairly compensated for schedule changes and overtime required

Clause Summaries and Drafting Notes

The model provisions that are included in these clauses cover the main concerns regarding work schedules and overtime including:

- ❏ The normal schedule and number of hours worked (is there a guaranteed number of hours

pay no matter how many hours worked)
- ❑ The typical work week (whether there are 8-hour shifts, 10-hour shifts, 12-hour shifts or some other normal work shift)
- ❑ Conditions for changing schedules or shifts
- ❑ Conditions under which an employee can be required to work overtime (mandatory or non-mandatory)
- ❑ How employees will be compensated for overtime work

The first version is a basic hours of work clause stating that employees will have at least eight hours off between shifts or be paid for time and a half for any hours worked with less than eight hours of a break. It also states when the schedule will be posted. These are relatively favorable clauses for the union.

The second version states that the normal workweek will be 40 hours and that overtime will be fairly distributed and that decisions regarding overtime will be subject to the grievance procedure. It provides a 14-day notice for the scheduling. It further provides that employees can change schedules with proper notice. Finally, it limits grievances on scheduling issues to the third step in which the management decision is final. This clause is reasonably favorable to management. Although it subjects scheduling decisions to the grievance procedure, it takes a "work first, grieve later" approach and limits appeals to the third step, where normally a final decision by management would be binding.

The third version is a relatively favorable provision for

management. It provides that while a typical workweek is 40 hours there is no guarantee. It provides for time and a half after 40 hours work in a week (this is the Federal law) and also states that lunch breaks will be unpaid.

The fourth version again states that the regular work schedule is eight hours a day and a 40-hour week, but gives the company the right to change that schedule when necessary. This provision provides for time and a half in excess of eight hours in a day. This is a relatively common provision in labor contracts and is over and above the requirement of Federal law for time and a half after 40 hours in a week. This clause also states that employees will be paid premium pay for work done on a Saturday (time and a half) and Sunday (double time). This clause is much more favorable to the union than some of the others.

The fifth version is basically concerned with the fairness in distribution of overtime. This is a somewhat uncommon provision in that it states that every three months the employer will look back at who has received overtime and will attempt to equalize overtime and rotate it among the employees in the department. This clause probably came out of a contract negotiation where there was a significant concern about favoritism in the awarding of overtime. Section 4 in this clause is interesting; it defines the term "similar" specifically. The parties clearly anticipated a dispute on this issue and attempted to clarify their intent within the agreement. This provision is a good example of how parties might negotiate very specific solutions to problems that arose during the administration of earlier contracts.

The final version provides for daily overtime after eight hours, as well as overtime after 40 hours in one week. This section is poorly drafted for the company; union members can clearly demand double overtime pay based on these two sections. Most agreements state that employees are only to be paid once for overtime in any pay period (i.e. if the employee works a normal 40 hour week except for working 10 hours on one day, that employee receives only 2 hours of overtime for the week as opposed to 2 hours overtime for working 10 hours in one day plus another 2 hours overtime for working 42 hours in one week). It also states that initially overtime will be assigned through the request of volunteers. If there are no volunteers overtime is assigned in reverse seniority order (least senior person receives the overtime assignment until all overtime assignments have been assigned). This provision also provides for show up pay on weekends (with a minimum of two hours pay) any time an employee is asked to come in off his regular shift, even if the employee only has to work for a short amount of time. Further, the provision allows for double time on Sundays. This provision is very favorable for the union.

Hours of Work/Overtime (version 1)
Section 1. The Company shall make every reasonable attempt to give employees eight (8) hours off between work assignments. If an employee is required to work with less than eight (8) hours rest, the Company agrees to pay time and one half for all hours short of the required eight (8) hours.
Section 2. Schedules will be prepared each Monday

for a period through the next eight days. This schedule will be subject to change due to additional requests, canceled requests, time changes, illness, or employees requesting not to work.

HOURS OF WORK/OVERTIME (version 2)
Section 1. Hours of Work and Overtime.
(A)   The normal workweek for each full-time employee shall be forty (40) hours.

(B)   Management retains the right to schedule its employees; however, the Company will make a good faith effort, whenever practical, to provide the employees with consecutive hours in the workday and consecutive days in the workweek.

(C)   The Company agrees that the assignment of overtime is not to be made on the basis of favoritism. In any case, where an employee has reason to believe that overtime is being assigned on the basis of favoritism, the employee shall have the right to the Grievance Procedure under Article 6 herein, to Step 3 of the procedure.

Section 2. Work Schedules, Vacation and Holiday Schedules.
(A)   When regular work schedules are changed, employees' normal work schedules, showing each employee's shift, workdays and hours, will be posted no less than fourteen (14) calendar days in advance, and will reflect at least a two (2) workweek schedule; however, the Company will make a good faith effort to reflect a one (1) month schedule. In the event an employee's shift, workdays or hours are changed while the employee is on approved leave the Company will make a good faith effort to notify the employee

of the change at his home. With prior written notification of at least three (3) workdays to the employee's immediate supervisor, employees may mutually agree to exchange days or shifts on a temporary basis. If the immediate supervisor objects to the exchange of workdays or shifts, the employee initiating the notification shall be advised that the exchange is disapproved.

(B)   Where practical, shifts, shift transfers and regular days off shall be scheduled with due regard for the needs of the Company, seniority and employee preference. The Company and the Union understand that there may be times when the needs of the Company will not permit such scheduling; however, when an employee's shift and/or regular days off are changed, the Company will make a good faith effort to keep the employee on the new shift or regular days off for a minimum of twelve (12) months unless otherwise requested by the employee.

(C)   When an employee is not assigned to a rotating shift and the employee's regular shift assignment is being changed, the Company will schedule the employee to be off work for a minimum of two shifts between the end of the previous shift assignment and the beginning of the new shift assignment.

(D)   Where practical, vacation and holiday leave shall be scheduled at least sixty (60) days in advance of such leave. Time off for vacations and holidays, when the holiday is a regularly scheduled workday for the employee, will be scheduled with due regard for the needs of the

Company, seniority and employee preference. In implementing this provision, nothing shall preclude the Company from making reasonable accommodations for extraordinary leave requests as determined by the Company or ensuring the fair distribution of leave during holidays.

(E)   A complaint concerning this Section may be grieved in accordance with Article 6 of this Agreement up to and including Step 3. The decision of the Step 3 Management Representative shall be final and binding on all parties.

Section 3. Rest Periods.

(A)   No supervisor shall unreasonably deny an employee a fifteen (15) minute rest period during each four (4) hour work shift. Whenever possible, such rest periods shall be scheduled at the middle of the work shift. However, it is recognized that many positions have an assignment that requires coverage for a full eight-hour shift, which would not permit the employee to actually leave his post. In those cases, it is recognized that the employee can "rest" while the employee physically remains in the geographic location of his duty post.

(B)   An employee may not accumulate unused rest periods, nor shall rest periods be authorized for covering an employee's late arrival on duty or early departure from duty.

Section 4. Non-Required Work Time. Bargaining unit employees shall not be required to volunteer time to the Company.

HOURS OF WORK/OVERTIME (version 3)
Section 1. The regular workweek shall be forty (40) hours per week. This provision shall in no way be construed as a guarantee by the Company of any amount of work in any period, or as a limitation of hours of work (including overtime) in any period.
Section 2. Employees shall be paid one and one half (1-1/2) times their regular straight time hourly rate for all hours worked in excess of forty (40) hours in one week.
Section 3. The Company shall schedule employees for a lunch break on the employee's own time.

HOURS OF WORK/OVERTIME (version 4)
Section 1. Starting times for bargaining unit employees shall be based on schedule needs. Employees may be required to report 30 minutes prior to scheduled departure times.
Section 2. The regular work schedule for all current bargaining unit employees shall be Monday-Friday. Any work on a sixth or seventh day shall be compensated in accordance with Section 6.
Section 3. The normal workday shall be eight (8) consecutive hours in any one work day, and the normal work week shall be forty (40) hours in any one week.
Section 4. Nothing in this Article shall prohibit the Company from changing starting times, ending times or scheduling work for different days when operationally necessary.
Section 5. All work in excess of eight (8) hours per day, or forty (40) hours per week, shall be paid for at the rate of time and one-half the regular base rate per hour for the number of hours worked.
Section 6. Any work performed on Saturdays shall be

paid for at the rate of one-and-one-half times the regular base rate per hour for the number of hours worked. All work performed on Sundays shall be paid double the regular base rate per hour for the number of hours worked.

Section 7. When necessary the Company may schedule more than eight (8) hours in any one workday, and more than forty (40) hours in any one work week, and the employee so scheduled agrees to meet the same.

HOURS OF WORK/OVERTIME (version 5)

Section 1. Insofar as practicable, overtime worked shall be equally divided among the employees in the crew and, pursuant to this policy, said overtime worked shall be rotated among said employees.

Section 2. Overtime and extra work in addition to the currently scheduled work week shall be divided on the basis of hours paid for, as impartially as possible, among employees in the same occupational group in the same department. Such impartial distribution need not take place in the same week but may be spread over a period of time.

Section 3. The foreman and the steward will jointly check the equalization of overtime and extra work lists at the end of each three-month period and wherever it is evident that certain employees are out of line so far as overtime and extra work is concerned, every effort will be made to give these employees the opportunity to be brought into line.

Section 4. The Employer agrees to rotate overtime within a department equally among employees working on similar work, provided that the employees are capable of performing the work for which overtime is required. The term "similar" being defined as work which can be performed by employees holding the same occupation and having the same caliber of skill within the occupation, in relation to the work for which overtime is necessary. Disputes as to the application of this clause shall be subject to the grievance procedure.

Section 5. Overtime shall be distributed as equally as possible among those who have earned seniority.

HOURS OF WORK/OVERTIME (version 6)

Section 1. Time and one half for all hours worked over 8 in a workday.

Section 2. Time and one half for all hours in pay status over 40 in the workweek.

Section 3. The Company will make its best effort to equalize overtime hours between Departments by year's end as much as practicable, on a rotating basis (August 16 through August 15 annually). If all employees refuse the overtime, such assignment will be made on an inverse seniority basis.

Section 4. By seniority, employees will be asked to fill in vacancies for other employees. If all employees refuse the overtime, such assignment will be made on an inverse seniority basis.

Section 5. Employees will not be charged for overtime when employee is on approved vacation, personal or illness leave, except when the request for leave is made after schedules are assigned.

Section 6. A minimum of two hours pay for any scheduled weekend trip. The employee must remain on duty for the two hours. Employees will receive the minimum of two (2) hours for any scheduled weekend trip cancelled less than 48 hours prior to the scheduled departure. The employee must report to work and remain on duty for the two hours.

Section 7.   Double time for all hours worked on the Sunday, provided the shift begins on Sunday. Hours worked as a continuation of a Saturday shift are considered Saturday hours and are not eligible for double time.

Vacation

Vacation benefits are regularly provided in union contracts. The main concern with employers and unions here, other than the financial impact of the vacation allotment, is how vacation time off is awarded and the circumstances under which vacation requests can be denied or modified based on the business needs of the company.

Clause Summaries and Drafting Notes

There are three model vacation clauses. The first version outlines the vacation entitlement and pro-rates vacation for employees during their first year of employment. It provides that employees will receive either their normal weekly pay or their average hours per week if they are part-time. It finally provides that payment will be prior to the employee going on vacation. This clause has no provisions for how vacations will be scheduled, and could be considered problematic for that reason (Are denials of vacation requests subject to the grievance procedure? When are vacation requests due? What happens when a low seniority employee requests a vacation slot also requested by a more senior employee?)

The second version states that seniority will be considered in deciding which conflicting vacation requests are approved. It states that the request must be made two months in advance and will be on a first come, first-served basis after that. This clause does not outline the accrual and suffers from some of the same limitations of clause one.

The third version provides table with the specific

accrual of vacation time based on length of service. In addition, it provides for eligibility and accumulation of vacation as well as payment for unused vacation on termination. This version also does not outline how conflicting requests or denials of requests are handled.

VACATIONS (version 1)

Section 1. Employees who meet the length of service and hours worked requirements calculated as of March 31 of each year receive paid vacation in accordance with the following schedule:

Length of Service Vacation Pay	Vacation Time Off
1 year 40 hours	1 week
5 years 80 hours	2 weeks
10 years 120 hours	3 weeks
20 years 160 hours	4 weeks

During the first year of service, employees will also be eligible for vacation based on the following proration schedule measured at March 31:

Length of Service Vacation Pay	Vacation Time Off
4 months & 690 hours 16 hours	2 days
6 months & 1040 hours 24 hours	3 days
8 months & 1380 hours 32 hours	4 days
10 months & 1739 hours 40 hours	5 days

An employee who has a work week of less than 8 hours per day, shall receive vacation pay based on the average amount of hours per week.

Section 2. Vacation pay shall be paid prior to employee's leave on vacation. Vacation pay shall be computed on a basis of 40 straight time hours for each week at the current hourly rate.

<u>VACATION (version 2)</u>

Section 1. Vacation requests will be granted by seniority when the request is made before two months prior to the first day of the month of the requested vacation.

Section 2. For vacation during the months in column one, request must be made by the date in column two:

January,	November 1
February,	December 1
March,	January 1
April,	February 1
May,	March 1
June,	April 1
July,	May 1
August,	June 1
September,	July 1
October,	August 1
November,	September 1
December,	October 1

Section 3. Vacation requests made after a deadline, will be honored on a first-come first-served basis.

VACATIONS (version 3)

Section 1. Vacation Accrual. Vacation accrues at the following rates depending on length of service with the Employer:

Length of Service	Days Accrued per Year	Maximum Accrual
0 through 4 years	10 days per year	20 days
5 through 9 years	15 days per year	30 days
10 through 14 years	18 days per year	36 days
15 through 19 years	20 days per year	40 days
20 through 24 years	22 days per year	44 days
25 years or more	25 days per year	50 days

Section 2. Eligibility. An employee must be employed for six (6) months before becoming eligible to take a vacation. Vacation accrues on a pay period basis. Vacation accrual may not accumulate beyond two (2) years. When employment is terminated, the employee's accumulated vacation will be paid.

Section 3. Accrual During Leaves of Absence. Vacation accrual will continue to accumulate during absence of an employee due to illness or injury to the extent of the accumulated sick leave, during an approved leave of absence for personal reasons and during the employee's vacation period. For occupational injuries, vacation accrual will continue to accumulate to the extent of State Industrial Accident Commission coverage or for a maximum of one (1) year. Anyone reemployed after resigning, insofar as vacation qualification is concerned, will be considered a new employee.

Leave of Absence
Leave of absence policies are another part of the
seniority compromise. There are several interests at
stake on leave of absence policies:

- ❑ The company has an interest in making sure it
  has a full complement of workers available to
  perform the necessary tasks of the business (i.e.
  under what circumstances can the company
  disapprove a leave of absence or otherwise take
  action to continue to operate its business
  without the employee's service?)
- ❑ The company also has a stake in providing leave
  for employees who are unavailable due to
  accident, injury or illness and to have an orderly
  procedure for employees to return to work when
  able
- ❑ The company also has legal obligations outside
  of the collective bargaining agreement that
  cannot be abrogated by the contract (FMLA,
  ADA, workers compensation, etc.)
- ❑ The union and its members (both those on leave
  of absence and those who remain behind) have a
  stake in what happens to an employee's seniority
  if they are away from the company for an
  extended period of time
- ❑ Employees who remain behind have a stake in
  when and under what conditions the absent
  employee loses his or her right to return,
  opening up a permanent job position

Clause Summaries and Drafting Notes
There are two model clauses that illustrate how
different companies and unions have dealt with this
compromise. It is important to remember that many of

these leave of absence policies are controlled by other federal and state rules (like the Family Medical Leave Act, the Americans with Disabilities Act, Uniformed Services Employment and Reemployment Rights Act, etc.) that can impact how an employer can deal with leave of absence policies.

The first version provides for leave of absence for up to 30 days with company approval required. It states that the reinstatement is based on the conditions in place at the time of the employee's return (this protects the employer in case of layoff or other business changes that occur during the term of the leave of absence). It states that the time on the leave of absence does not count seniority for the wage progression. This basic clause is relatively favorable and open-ended for the employer.

The second version is a very pro-management clause that simply states that the employer's policies will control on family medical leaves of absence and incorporates the company policy into the contract. One of the key questions that comes up in a clause like this is whether the company has the right to change its policy during the term of the contract since there is one specific policy that is incorporated by reference at the time the contract is entered. This typically is more of a management's rights clause issue although the language of the contract provision can make clear that the company has the right to change its policies mid-term. This particular clause does not do so.

LEAVE OF ABSENCE (version 1)
Section 1. Upon written application from an

employee, the Company may grant a written leave of absence without pay where good cause is shown for a period not to exceed thirty (30) days. The leave may be extended or renewed for additional periods of thirty (30) days for reasons which, in the opinion of the Company, are satisfactory.

Section 2. An employee returning from a leave of absence shall be reinstated subject to the conditions prevailing at the time of his return. Reinstatement is not guaranteed.

Section 3. Eligibility for, and accrual towards, Company benefits while an employee is on leave of absence shall be determined by Company policy, said determination to be within the judgment of the Company. Time off on leave of absence shall not be counted toward advancement to the next wage progression step.

Leave of Absence (version 2)

The provisions of the Family and Medical Leave Act will be incorporated into this Agreement. Administration of such leave will be in accord with the procedures set forth in Appendix "_____" of this Agreement.

Drug and Alcohol Testing

Drug and alcohol testing is an increasingly common provision in collective bargaining agreements. Although initially a significant area of contention in contracts (and occasionally still very contentious—like the issue of steroid testing in the professional baseball contract) these provisions are more common today. Unions sometimes oppose drug and alcohol testing for members, particularly where the testing is in the control of the company. However, many organizations are covered by laws that require them to drug test, for example the Drug Free Workplace Act for government contractors and department of transportation regulations for companies in the transportation industry.

The basic interests at stake in these clauses are the following:

- ❑ The productivity, safety and human costs of drug addiction in the workplace
- ❑ The legal requirements for regulated companies
- ❑ The management rights issue of controlling how drug tests will be administered (control over costs, chain of custody, privacy)
- ❑ The union's interest in making sure employees are treated fairly and compassionately (treatment, "last chance" provisions, ensuring testing handled professionally and accurately, etc.)

Clause Summaries and Drafting Notes

There are two model clauses on drug testing below. The primary elements of the drug and alcohol testing compromise are in the following areas:

- What substances are tested (drugs only, drugs and alcohol)?
- What amounts will result in a "positive" result? (most labs use standard cutoffs, but sometimes these limits are different – DOT levels are sometimes different that normal testing limits)
- How are tests administered (in-house nurse, outside contractor)?
- How is chain of custody maintained and controlled?
- Are positive test samples re-tested?
- How is the employee notified (privacy concerns) and is the employee given an opportunity to refute or explain a positive test result?
- What happens to an employee who tests positive? Are they immediately terminated, referred to treatment, given a "last chance" agreement, subject to additional testing?

The first model clause is a very simple and pro-management version. It simply states that the company's drug testing policy will control. It incorporates the company policy by reference. The clause does not state whether the company can change its policy during the term of the contract and this particular provision does not seem to indicate that that policy can change. To avoid arbitrations on this point the company and the union could agree to language that specifically prohibits changes during the term of the contract or allows for changes during the term of the contract.

The second version is a more favorable clause for the union and provides that drug testing will occur according to the Drug Free Workplace Act. It does provide for random testing for "special risk" categories of workers covered by the Department of Transportation, which is required by regulation. The clause does provide that the grievance policy applies to disciplinary action caused by the testing policy. Finally, it provides a claim procedure for lost property during drug searches. This last provision was probably something of a local concern that is not common in general drug testing provisions.

DRUG AND ALCOHOL TESTING (version 1)

The Company's Drug and Alcohol Testing Program will be applicable to employees covered by this Agreement. This Program is set forth as Appendix "_____." [Note: For examples of drug and alcohol testing policies, see my website at http://www.lrims.com/Policyhome.htm]

DRUG AND ALCOHOL TESTING (version 2)

Section 1. The Company and the Union agree to drug testing of bargaining unit employees in accordance with the Drug-Free Workplace Act. In accordance with the Company Drug and Alcohol Testing Policy, all employees shall be subject to random drug testing.
Section 2. Special risk classes for drug testing purposes within the bargaining unit are denoted by an asterisk in Appendix A. Special risk means employees who are required as a condition of employment to be certified under Department of Transportation or other regulations.
Section 3. An employee shall have the right to grieve any disciplinary action taken under the Drug and Alcohol Testing Policy. If an employee is not disciplined but is denied a demotion, reassignment or promotion

as a result of a positive confirmed drug test, the employee shall have the right to grieve such action in accordance with the Grievance Procedure.

Section 4. Any searches conducted of employees shall be in accordance with the Drug and Alcohol Testing Policy.

Section 5. If an employee's personal property suffers damage or destruction in the course of a drug search on the Company's property, the employee may submit a claim for reimbursement under the provisions of Article Replacement of Personal Property.

National Health Care Program

Most observers believe that the health care delivery system in America today is getting unsustainable; from spiraling costs of care and prescription drugs to the related expenses of health insurance, many working class and retired Americans are clamoring for change. During the first term of the Clinton administration, and even during the 2004 presidential primaries, there was discussion in Washington about nationalizing or making significant changes to the way health insurance and health benefits are provided.

A major purpose of contract language is to provide certainty over issues where there is uncertainty. For this reason, contracts will sometime discuss how to deal with a situation that is foreseeable, but not in any detailed way—national healthcare is such a situation. Since unions and companies can foresee that a significant change in the health care system is at least a remote possibility during the 3 to 7 year term of most labor contracts, they may want language that indicates what the parties will do if that happens.

Clause Summaries and Drafting Notes

Since the details of a national health program are so uncertain, most parties just want to keep open the possibility to re-negotiate over the issue in the future. That is what the model clause here does. If either party wanted to further clarify this language, they could more carefully define what counts as a National Health Care Plan, as well as what happens if no agreement can be reached upon re-opening the contract.

NATIONAL HEALTH CARE PROGRAM

In the event that a National Health Care Plan shall become law, this Agreement may be re-opened for the purposes of negotiating on health care issues only (Article ___). The party requesting re-opening shall give written notice thereof to the other party and negotiations shall commence within fifteen (15) calendar days of such notice.

Bereavement Leave

Bereavement leave is a benefit that is often offered by organizations, usually for the death of an immediate family member. There are two sample clauses below. The basic interests at stake here are the details of the benefit (the amount of time off, whether the leave is paid or not, the family members for which bereavement pay is provided) and the company's discretion in implementing it.

Clause Summaries and Drafting Notes

There are two model clauses. They are each relatively straightforward. The first clause is somewhat more expansive than the second since it allows one day of leave for the death of in-laws. The second version provides up to 3 days of paid leave including the day of the funeral plus one day after the funeral to return.

BEREAVEMENT LEAVE (version 1)

Funeral leave up to three (3) regular scheduled working days with pay at the straight time rate shall be given an employee in case of death of his mother, father, step-mother, step-father, sister, brother, wife, husband, son, daughter or grandparent to attend funeral services. In case of death of a mother-in-law, father-in-law, brother-in-law or sister-in-law, one (1) day leave with pay will be granted to attend the funeral. The Company retains the right to request verification of the death.

BEREAVEMENT LEAVE (version 2)

An employee will be assured against loss of pay due to death in immediate family (mother, father, step-mother, step-father, sister, brother, wife, husband, son, daughter or grandparent) up to three (3) days.

This assurance is only to apply up to and including the day of funeral; however, in cases where extended travel is involved to the funeral, the following day will also be included.

Jury Duty Pay
Companies are required in most states to compensate employees for time spent on a jury. Some employers will in addition provide benefits for employees who are subpoenaed to testify in a trial.

Clause Summaries and Drafting Notes
The basic issues here are the rate of pay and whether the employee is required to pay back money paid by the court itself. Secondary issues include whether employees can receive paid time off when subpoenaed to testify in a trial (especially if it is a trial in which they are a party–if not careful the company could end up paying an employee to testify in a trial against the company!)

There are two versions here. The first version provides for 8 hours pay per day and requires that the employee pay the company all they receive from the court except for expenses. The clause also requires the employee to report for work on any day in which they are excused from jury duty. This clause is relatively limited and is more common to labor contracts.

The second version provides for pay at the regular rate of pay for jury duty or if summoned to appear in court as a result of their job or if required by a federal, state or local government subpoena. This clause is more expansive and could potentially allow an employee to receive pay for a lawsuit in which they are a party. It requires that the employee repay the employer any money received except for expenses and it also requires the employee to report to a supervisor for work if they are off of jury duty for over four hours during a regularly scheduled work shift.

JURY DUTY PAY (version 1)
Section 1. An employee who is called for jury duty will be excused from work for such duty after presenting to his supervisor the Summons for such duty. The Company will pay the employee his normal straight time hourly rate for a maximum of eight (8) hours for each such day lost from regularly scheduled work. In order to receive jury duty pay, the employee will be required to pay to the Company any and all remunerations received for jury service; however, he may keep such payments as are deemed to be an expense allowance.

Section 2. In order to qualify for the benefits provided herein, an employee called for jury duty must report for work at his usual starting time if he is excused from appearing in court for any full day. Moreover, he must promptly report for work whenever his presence is not required on the jury for any time falling within his regular working hours.

JURY DUTY PAY (version 2)
Section 1. The Employer shall pay the employee's regular straight time hourly rate when an employee is required to serve on jury duty or is subpoenaed to appear as a witness as a result of the employee's job, or as the result of a subpoena by federal, state or local government. The employee must endorse and remit to the Employer all monies received for such service (witness fees, jury duty pay, etc.), except the mileage allowance.

Section 2. If an employee reports to the court and is notified that the employee will not be called, or if the employee is excused after serving less than four (4) hours, the employee is to report to the employee's supervisor for possible work assignment.

Safety

Labor contracts regularly contain clauses regarding safety at the company. Most begin with a joint statement regarding the mutual commitment of the company and the union to protect the safety of workers. While this may sound cynical, this mutual commitment is not what these clauses are about.

The main issue behind these clauses is the division of responsibility for safety in the plant and clarification of how employees may be disciplined for safety infractions. Typically the company will want strict disciplinary authority for safety violations. Like with other serious infractions (discrimination, fighting or threats of violence, harassment) the company may attempt to remove those questions outside of the grievance process. They will argue that they are obligated under a federal and state law to protect the safety of workers (under laws like the Occupational and Safety Health Act) and for that reason need wider latitude enforcing and implementing safety requirements.

Unions on the other hand will want to maintain control over the disciplinary action process. While unions will agree to a point to help the company promote safety in the workplace, the union will want to ensure that members are not unfairly disciplined through the use of the company's broader authority under the safety clause. For this reason, unions will object to removing disciplinary action for safety violations from the grievance procedure. While they obviously share a concern over safe work conditions for members (it is after all these same members who are injured if a plant is unsafe) they typically feel their obligation to protect members from unfair discipline or discharge is more important than giving management broad powers to enforce safety standards.

Clause Summaries and Drafting Notes

The basic issues outlined in most safety clauses are the following:

- A statement regarding the company and union's joint commitment to safety
- Clarification about how safety standards will be communicated to members (usually as a stand-alone safety rules incorporated by reference, but sometimes specifically listed in the contract)
- Employer's authority to discipline workers for violations of safety standards, and whether that is subject to the grievance procedure
- Whether the company or members are required to provide and maintain safety equipment
- The member's obligation to report safety violations or unsafe work conditions
- The creation or use of a safety committee

There are three model safety clauses. The first version creates a duty for employees to report unsafe working conditions and states that the employer is not allowed to require employees to perform work that is reasonably believed unsafe. Finally, it provides for physical exams to be paid for by the company. This clause is relatively favorable to the union since it gives employees the right in the contract to refuse to work where they "reasonably" believe a condition to be unsafe. Often this is in the eye of the beholder, and it may be difficult to deal with in an arbitration case.

The second version is a simple safety clause essentially establishing the authority for the employer to create a safety committee. It also includes a provision requiring notification of the employer in any case where a safety problem arises. Finally, it establishes that grievances regarding enforcement of safety rules and procedures are only grievable through step 3 of the grievance process; in other words they are not eligible for arbitration in the employer's final response in the third step of the grievance process is final and binding on the union. This clause is more favorable to the company, giving it wider latitude to discipline recidivist offenders of safety standards.

The third version also establishes a safety committee. It requires the employer to furnish safety equipment and states that the company will reimburse employees for such equipment. It requires the employer to notify the union of any lost time accidents on the day that those accidents occur. It also provides for payment to employees for the remainder of their shift on days are involved in a lost time accident. The clause further provides for sanitation, ventilation, and breathing respiration equipment. Finally, it provides for employer paid physical exams. This clause again is relatively pro-union, in that it states many obligations for the company, but few for the union or its members.

SAFETY (version 1)
Section 1. The Employer recognizes its responsibility to make all reasonable provisions for the health and safety of the employees, to assure and enforce compliance with Federal and State laws, and to

maintain sound operating practices that will result in safe working conditions.

Section 2. The Union recognizes the responsibility of its members to obey reasonable safety rules and follow safe work practices to insure employee safety as well as that of fellow workers.

Section 3. An employee shall immediately report any unsafe working condition or work practice to the immediate supervisor.

Section 4. The Employer shall not require employees to work in unsafe and unhealthful environments.

Section 5. The Company and Union agree to require physical examinations and qualifications for bargaining unit employees. The Company will pay for such examinations at a medical facility of its choosing.

SAFETY (version 2)

Section 1. Safety Committee. It shall be the policy of the Company to make every reasonable effort to provide employees a safe and healthy working environment. Unit employees shall select at least one person from each department to serve on a safety committee.

Section 2. Employee Safety.

(A)   Any employee becoming aware of a work-related accident shall immediately notify the supervisor of the area where the incident occurred.

(B)   When an employee believes that an unsafe working condition exists in the work area, the employee shall immediately report the condition to the supervisor. The supervisor shall investigate the report and make a reasonable effort to take action deemed appropriate.

Section 3. Grievability. Complaints which arise under the application or interpretation of this Article shall be grievable, but only up to Step 3 of the Grievance Procedure of the Agreement.

SAFETY (version 3)
Section 1. Safe Working Conditions, Working Safely. The Employer will exert every reasonable effort to provide and maintain safe working conditions, and the Union will cooperate to that end and support the employer when discipline is required in the case of flagrant or repeated safety regulation violations. The Union will encourage their members to work in a safe manner.

Section 2. Safety Committee. To that end, the [State] Occupational Safety and Health Code as amended shall apply for safety committee formation, membership, duties, functions, training and instruction.

Section 3. Safety Shoes, Glasses, Hardhats, Injuries, Licensing Fees.

(A)   The Employer shall furnish suitable equipment for the protection of workers' eyes. Employees shall wear safety equipment as required.

(B)   The Employer shall furnish hard hats, safety glasses, ear muffs or ear plugs and employees shall wear them as required.

(C)   The Employer will reimburse the employee for the basic, reasonable replacement cost of prescription safety glasses if said glasses are ruined or broken on the job.

(D)   The Employer will reimburse employees for safety shoes, to a maximum of Seventy-five dollars ($75.00) per contract year. The employee must present a receipt for the safety shoes to the Maintenance Operations Manager prior to the reimbursement. The annual allowance of $75.00 may be carried over one year to a maximum of $150.00 if the employee has not been reimbursed for safety shoes during the previous year. Employees shall wear safety shoes as required.

(E)   An employee suffering an industrial injury who is advised not to resume work by a nurse, first aid attendant or by a physician to whom the employee has been referred shall be paid on the employee's usual basis, pursuant to the terms of this Agreement, to the end of the shift on which the injury occurred. If such employee reports such injury immediately following its occurrence to the nurse, first aid attendant or physician designated by the Employer and completes working the shift during which the employee was so injured and on the following day, after reporting for work, is advised by the nurse, first aid attendant or physician, to whom the employee has been referred by the Employer, not to continue work because of said injury, the employee shall be paid to the end of said shift.

(F)   The Employer shall notify the respective Union not later than the end of the working day, if possible, of any lost time accidents to any of its members that necessitated confinement in any hospital or clinic, provided the Employer has knowledge of such confinement.

(G)   The Employer shall furnish protective clothing as necessary. The Employer will provide rubber boots at the employee's request for those employees required to use foliage spraying equipment.

(H)   The Employer will reimburse One Hundred percent (100.0%) of the cost of licensing fees for any craft when the Employer requires the employee to have a license or certification. The employee must present a receipt for the license or certificate to the Maintenance Operations Manager prior to reimbursement.

Section 4. Sanitation.

(A)   Suitable lockers, washrooms and drinking water shall be furnished by the Employer.

(B)   All toilets and washrooms shall be kept in a clean and sanitary condition, properly heated and ventilated, and adequate quarters, with heat and hot water, shall be provided for employees to change and dry their clothes. Lunch areas with benches and tables shall be provided and shall be separate from toilet facilities.

Section 5. Ventilation. Where noxious or poisonous gases may accumulate, the Employer shall provide proper protection and ventilation. Proper lighting and ventilation shall be provided for all enclosed working spaces. No spray painting shall be performed in confined spaces without adequate ventilation and use of respirators.

Section 6. Physical Examination. The Employer may require a medical examination when the employee's ability to physically perform the required work is in question, or where an employee's performance might jeopardize the life and health of the employee or co-workers. The Employer may also require a physical examination if it is necessary to acquire or maintain a license in order to perform the duties of the job. If the physical exam is for the purpose of obtaining or maintaining a required license, employees may elect to go to a physician of their choice. Upon receipt of the medical exam report, the Company will reimburse employees up to the amount normally paid to the Company's contracted physicians. The Employer agrees to defend and hold harmless, to the extent permitted by law, the Union, its officers and agents from any liability arising out of the application or administration of this provision. No provision of this contract shall in any way limit the Americans with Disabilities Act of 1990.

Grievance Procedure

One of the most important clauses in any labor agreement is the grievance procedure. This clause gives employees and their union representatives a procedure to follow in order to appeal disciplinary action or enforcement of work rules with which they do not agree. There are several key interests at stake between management and the union in reaching the grievance process compromise:

- The grievance process compromise is the ultimate abdication of management rights authority to the union–the core issue is how much of that management rights authority the company is willing to cede to the union
- Who has final authority to decide grievances? This is the fundamental compromise, and it is usually (but not always) an outside neutral
- What can be arbitrated? This defines the issues the parties are willing to leave in the hands of an outsider
- What remedies are available to (or removed from) the arbitrator?
- Under what circumstances are otherwise legitimate complaints outside the jurisdiction of the arbitrator? Things like missed time limits and clauses which specifically prohibit appeal to the grievance procedure are the most common
- What procedures will be followed? The exact steps, time-limits and other procedures will affect how efficiently cases are decided and, in many cases, will help determine the winner or loser of a specific grievance

Clause Summaries and Drafting Notes

Grievance clauses are typically among the longest and most detailed clauses in any labor agreement. There are a number of critical issues that are a part of virtually every grievance process clause.

Number of Steps. The first key feature of any grievance procedure is the number of steps a grievance must follow to be resolved and at what step a decision becomes final and binding on the parties. The number of steps is less important than when it becomes final; the most important question is who reaches that decision. Most grievance procedures require between three and four steps. They generally begin with either an oral presentation of the grievance or a more formal written presentation of the grievance to an immediate supervisor or sometimes a department head regarding the issue at hand.

The second step of the grievance is typically appealed to either a higher-level manager or possibly to a human resources department representative. A normal third step is appeal to the top manager at the local level or sometimes to a corporate level labor relations representative. Occasionally there will be additional steps (to a higher-level labor relations or human resources representative or possibly even the company president). The final step in most grievance procedures is an appeal to arbitration, either to an individual arbitrator or to a panel of arbitrators.

Time Limits. The next important part of the grievance procedure is the time limits involved. Most grievance procedures require complaints to be filed within a limited period of time after the incident that gave rise to the grievance occurs or reasonably should have been known to the grievant. Each step of the grievance procedure will also have its own separate time limitation for appeal. Typically, the grievance process will penalize the grievant for failing to appeal the grievance prior to the expiration of the appeal period. Most of the time this penalty is the waiver of any additional appeal right.

Many grievance procedures also state that if a company fails to respond to an employee prior to the conclusion of the appeal period that the company is presumed to have denied the grievance and the grievant must appeal the company's decision within the timeframe provided. This is not always the case; sometimes unions will get companies to agree that if they fail to deny the grievance within the time limits provided that the grievant wins the grievance. In other cases, a failure to appeal within the timeframe provided just sends the appeal to the next step.

<u>Final Authority</u>. Next the grievance procedure will identify who has final authority to decide the grievance. Generally, that final authority is granted to an arbitrator or panel of arbitrators chosen through some neutral process. Some grievance clauses will also outline the arbitration procedure. In this text I have separated the two (which is also common). For a full discussion of arbitration clauses see that chapter.

Below are five examples of grievance procedures. The first version is a relatively limited three-step appeal process. Grievances that are not appealed within the time limits are considered denied and no longer eligible for appeal. Further, appeal is only to the company president whose decision is final and binding and there is no recourse to an outside arbitrator or other neutral. Time spent in the grievance process is not work-time and the clause prohibits the solicitation of grievances. This clause is among the most pro-management you will find, and is not that much different from the "open door" dispute resolution process common in most non-union companies.

The second version is a four-step process that has an opposite view of the expiration of time limits, stating that when the time limit expires it gives either party the right to appeal to the next step in the process. It states that there is no retroactive relief for more than 20 days prior to the written grievance and there is also a reference to a separate and distinct arbitration clause that is not included in the grievance procedure (there are several examples of these clauses later in the book). This clause is much more favorable to the union and its members.

The third version defines the parties and states that grievances will be informal prior to the third step of the grievance process; they are required to be in writing after step 3. The procedure also defines what counts as a "work day" and provides that employees can proceed with grievances with or without union representation–however they cannot use an attorney. The expiration of a time limit provides a right to appeal. The fourth step of the process is up to the director of labor relations and then can be appealed through a separate arbitration procedure defined in another clause. This clause strikes a "middle ground" common to many grievance procedures.

The fourth version is enormously detailed and unwieldy, with very extended time-limits. It gives grievant the opportunity to "opt out" of the procedure at the beginning, otherwise the union's decision is final and binding on the employee. It limits time-off allowed for the investigation of grievances. It also states that the settlements before the third step will not be binding precedents. This "past practice" limitation may not be followed, however; most arbitrators rely heavily on the history between the parties to decide grievances. This clause contains language favorable to both sides, but is also very complicated and time-consuming. It keeps disputes unresolved for extended periods, and could potentially result in large back-pay liability for the company.

The fifth and last version provides disciplinary action for just cause and requires a seven-day suspension without pay prior to any discharge. It requires notification of the union in the case of any discharge and a 5-day time limit for the appeal for non-disciplinary actions. There is a 3-step grievance procedure along with arbitration. This process also defines an ultimate striking procedure for the selection of arbitrators. This clause, overall, is probably more favorable to the union (particularly the requirement of the suspension prior to any discharge decision).

GRIEVANCE PROCEDURE (version 1)
Section 1. A grievance within the meaning of the Article shall be limited to a dispute arising between the parties hereto involving interpretation of application of

the provisions of this Agreement. Should a grievance arise it shall be handled in the following manner:

Step 1. The aggrieved employee will present his grievance to his immediate supervisor within two (2) working days of the occurrence of the complained-of event. If not presented within this period of time, the case cannot be presented at a future date. The Company shall render a decision within seven (7) working days of the date of presentation.

Step 2. If not disposed of in Step 1, the employee may present the grievance in writing to the Company. A decision at Step 1 shall be considered to be final and the grievance shall be considered to be withdrawn unless the grievance is taken to Step 2 within three (3) working days of the date of decision at Step 1. The Company shall give this decision within seven (7) working days after the grievance is presented to him.

Step 3. If not disposed of in Step 2, the employee and the business representative of the Union may appeal the grievance by giving written notice thereof to the Company. A decision at Step 2 shall be considered as final unless the notice of appeal to Step 3 is given within five (5) calendar days after the decision. The Company shall render this decision within seven (7) calendar days from the date the written grievance is presented at Step 3.

At any step of the grievance procedure, if the appropriate Company representative does not act within the specified period of time, the grievance shall be considered as having been denied as of conclusion of the applicable time period.

Section 2. Only those issues fulfilling both of the following requirements can be appealed beyond Step 3.

(A)   The grievance must be based on an alleged violation by the Company of a specific contract provision or must be based on the interpretation or application of a specific provision of the contract. A Company decision will not be subject to reversal unless it is found that the Company misinterpreted or violated the express terms of the contract.

(B)   The grievance must have been processed through each step of the grievance procedure in a timely manner unless it has been mutually agreed in writing by both parties that a specific step is to be bypassed or time limits waived.

Section 3. If the decision of the Company in Step 3 is unsatisfactory to the Union, and the Union wishes to process the grievance further, the Union must make a written request to the Company within seven (7) calendar days following the Step 3 decision. The written request shall include a specific statement of the violations and the position of the Union concerning the Union's interpretation of the disputed contract provision along with the specific remedy requested.

Section 4. Appeal of a Step 3 decision shall be to the President of the Company who shall have the final authority to render a decision on the matter. The decision of the President shall be final and binding upon the Company, its employees, and Union; provided, however, in no event shall any decision to be made retroactive prior to the two (2) calendar day period referred in Step 1 of the Grievance Procedure.

Section 5. All grievance matters shall be handled at a time other than normal working hours, and shall not interfere with an employee's performance of his duties. Time spent by the employees in handling such matters shall be without pay.

Section 6. No employee or Union representative shall in any manner solicit or encourage grievances and disputes. Any grievance or dispute which has been in any way solicited or encouraged shall be null and void, will be reviewed by the Company for such reason, and will not be subject to the grievance procedure.

GRIEVANCE PROCEDURE (version 2)

Section 1. The purpose of this article is to provide an orderly method for the settlement of a dispute between the parties over the interpretation, application, or claimed violation of any of the provisions of this agreement. Such a dispute shall be defined as a grievance under this agreement and must be presented promptly (or within 5 working days after it arises) and be processed in accordance with the following steps, time limits, and conditions herein set forth. The parties agree that pending the raising, processing, and settlement of a grievance, and during the term of this agreement, there shall be no slowdown, stoppage, or other interference with work or plant operations, as provided for in Article [The No-Strike, No-Lockout Provision] of this agreement.

>Step 1. The employee shall first take up his grievance with his immediate foreman; and if the aggrieved employee requests, the shop steward in his department shall be given an opportunity to be present at a time to be fixed by the foreman. If the grievance is not settled, it shall within three working days thereafter be set forth in writing, signed by the employee, and

given to the foreman, who shall within three working days after receipt thereof give his written answer to the grievance.

Step 2. If the grievance is not settled in Step 1, the union may appeal it by giving a written notice of such appeal within five working days after receipt of the foreman's written answer to the department superintendent (or section or area head), who shall discuss it with the union's Grievance Committee at a time to be fixed by the department superintendent or his designated representative. The department superintendent or his designated representative shall give his written answer to the grievance within five working days after the close of the discussion.

Step 3. If the grievance is not settled in Step 2, the union may appeal it by giving a written notice of such appeal within seven working days after receipt of the answer of the department superintendent or his designated representative to the plant manager, who shall discuss it with the union's international representative (or business agent) and the union's Grievance Committee at a time to be fixed by the plant manager or his designated representative. The plant manager or his designated representative shall give his written answer to the grievance within ten working days after the close of the discussion.

Step 4. If the grievance is not settled in Step 3, it may be appealed by a written notice of such appeal given by the union to the company within ten working days after the receipt of the written answer of the plant manager or his designated representative to arbitration in accordance with the procedure and conditions set forth in the arbitration clause hereinafter set forth.

Section 2. The parties agree to follow each of the foregoing steps in the processing of the grievance; and if at any step the company's representative fails to give his written answer within the time limit therein set forth, the union may appeal the grievance to the next step at the expiration of such time limit.

Section 3. The settlement of a grievance in any case shall not be made retroactive for a period exceeding twenty working days prior to the date the grievance was first presented in writing.

Section 4. If the company claims that the union has violated the no-strike clause of this agreement, it may present such claim to the union in writing; and if the parties fail to settle it, the company may appeal it to arbitration, in accordance with the arbitration clause hereinafter set forth.

GRIEVANCES (version 3)

Section 1. A grievance shall be defined as any dispute or difference between the parties with respect to the application, administration and interpretation of the provisions of this Agreement. All grievances shall be filed in accordance with the provisions herein. The grievant may be an employee, group of employees or the Union. Grievances filed by the Union shall be initiated in writing at step 3 of the grievance process within 5 working days after the Union becomes aware or should have been aware through the use of reasonable diligence of the circumstances or conditions causing the grievance. For purposes of the grievance procedure, workdays are considered to be Monday through Friday.

Section 2. An employee may choose to pursue a grievance with or without representation. Obtaining representation shall be totally the responsibility of the employee. An employee representative, other than an attorney, may be involved with the employee at any step within the grievance procedure.

Section 3. The time limits herein set forth may be extended by mutual consent of both parties if submitted in writing to the General Manager's designated representative for steps 1 through 3 or to the Corporate Labor Relations designated representative for step 4. If at any step within the grievance procedure the Employer fails to respond within the time limits herein set forth, the grievant may appeal the grievance to the next step within 5 working days.

Section 4. The grievance process shall be administered according to the following procedure.

Step 1. Within five (5) working days after the first occurrence, or within five (5) working days after the grievant becomes aware or should have been aware through the use of reasonable diligence of the circumstances or conditions causing the grievance, the grievant shall orally present the grievance to the immediate supervisor. The immediate supervisor shall provide an oral response within 5 working days after such presentation.

Step 2. If the grievance is not settled at Step 1 and the grievant wishes to appeal the grievance to Step 2, the grievance and the Step 1 response shall be reduced to writing and signed by the grievant and the immediate supervisor. The written grievance shall contain a complete statement of the facts, the provision or provisions of this Agreement at issue and the relief requested. The written grievance shall be submitted to the department head within 5 workdays of the immediate supervisor's oral response. The department head shall meet with the grievant in an attempt to resolve the grievance at a time mutually agreeable to the parties. The department head's response shall be reduced to writing within 5 workdays following the meeting.

Step 3. If the grievance is not settled at Step 2 and the grievant wishes to appeal the grievance to Step 3, the grievance shall be submitted in writing to the Labor Relations Manager within 5 work days after the department head's written response. The Labor Relations Manager shall schedule a meeting between his/her representative and the grievant at the time mutually agreeable to the parties. The Labor Relations Manager shall issue a written response to the grievance within 10 workdays following the meeting.

Step 4. If the grievance is not settled at Step 3 and the grievant wishes to appeal the grievance to Step 4, the grievance shall be submitted within 10 work days to the Director of Labor Relations. The Director of Labor Relations shall schedule a meeting with the grievant at a time mutually agreeable to the parties. The Director of Labor Relations shall issue a written response to the grievance within 15 calendar days of the meeting, unless the time frame is extended by mutual agreement. If the Grievance is not settled at this step the parties may appeal the final decision of the Director of Labor Relations under the arbitration procedure outlined in Article ___.

GRIEVANCES (version 4)

It is the policy of the Company and Union to encourage informal discussions between supervisors and employees of employee complaints. Such discussions should be held with view to reaching an understanding, which will resolve the matter in a manner satisfactory to the employee without need for recourse to the formal grievance procedure prescribed by this Article.

Section 1. Definitions. As used in this Article:

(A) "Grievance" shall mean a dispute involving the interpretation or application of the specific provisions of this Agreement, except as exclusions are noted in this Agreement.

(B) "Employee" shall mean an individual employee or a group of employees having the same grievance. In the case of a group of employees one employee shall be designated by the group to act as spokesperson and to be responsible for processing the grievance.

(C) "Days" shall mean calendar days, excluding any day observed as a holiday pursuant to the Personnel Rules of the Career Service System, or holiday observed by the Union pursuant to a list furnished the Company in writing, as of the effective date of this Agreement.

Section 2. Election of Remedy and Representation.

(A) An employee who decides to use this Grievance Procedure shall indicate at the Oral Step or initial written step (if authorized by the provisions of this Article) whether or not he shall be represented by the Union. If the employee is represented by the Union, any decision mutually agreed to by the Company and Union shall be binding on the employee.

(B)   Where Union representation is requested by an employee, the employee's representative shall be selected from the list of Union Grievance Representatives or Union Staff Representatives which has been provided to the Company by the Union.

(C)   When an employee has been appropriately designated to serve as a Grievance Representative and the Company has been notified in accordance with Section 2, Paragraph (B), the Grievance Representative shall be authorized to investigate grievances and represent grievant in accordance with this Article, subject to the following limitations:

    a. A Grievance Representative will not be allowed time off with pay to investigate his own grievance.

    b. Time spent by a Grievance Representative in investigating a grievance shall be the minimum amount of time necessary to perform the specific investigation involved.

        i. If an employee selects a Grievance Representative to represent him in a grievance which has been properly filed in accordance with this Article, the Grievance Representative may be allowed a reasonable amount of annual or compensatory leave to investigate the grievance at the Oral Step and to represent the grievant at any Oral Step and Step 1 meetings which are held during regular work hours. Such annual or compensatory leave shall be subject to prior approval by the Grievance Representative's immediate supervisor; however, approval of such time off will not be withheld, if the Grievance Representative can be allowed such time off without interfering with, or unduly hampering the operations of the unit to which the Grievance Representative is regularly assigned. The Grievance Representative's immediate supervisor will notify the grievant's supervisor prior to allowing the Grievance Representative time off to investigate the grievance.

ii. Investigations will be conducted in a way that does not interfere with Company operations.

iii. The Grievance Representative must be selected from those Grievance Representatives within the same work unit as the grievant's work unit. If no Grievance Representative is located in the grievant's work unit, the Grievance Representative must be selected from the work unit which is located closest to the grievant's work location.

    iv. A Grievance Representative who has been selected to represent an employee as provided in this Article, will be considered a required participant at the Step 1 grievance meeting.

(D)   Both the employee and the employee's representative, if any, shall be notified of the Step 1 meeting. Further, all communication concerning written grievances or their resolution shall be in writing and a copy shall be sent to both the employee and the employee's representative.

(E)   If the employee is not represented by the Union, any adjustment of the grievance shall be consistent with the terms of this Agreement, the Union shall be given reasonable opportunity to be present at any meeting called for the resolution of the grievance, and processing of the grievance will be in accordance with the procedures established in this Agreement. The Union shall not be bound by the decision of any grievance in which the employee chose not to be represented by the Union.

(F)   The resolution of a grievance prior to its submission in writing at Step 3 shall not establish a precedent binding on either the Company or the Union in other cases.

Section 3. Procedures.

(A)   Employee grievances filed in accordance with

this Article should be presented and handled promptly at the lowest level of supervision having the authority to adjust the grievances.

(B) Once a grievance is presented, no new violation or issue can be raised.

(C) There shall be no reprisals against any of the participants in the procedures contained herein by reason of such participation.

(D) If a grievance meeting is held or requires reasonable travel time during the working hours of any required participant, such participant shall be excused without loss of pay for that purpose. Attendance at grievance meetings outside of regular working hours shall not be deemed time worked.

(E) Grievances shall be presented and adjusted in the following manner, and no one individual may respond to a grievance at more than one written step.

    a. Oral Discussion

        i. An employee having a grievance may, within fourteen (14) days following the occurrence of the event giving rise to the grievance, present the grievance orally to the Oral Step representative. The Oral Step representative shall make every effort to resolve the grievance at the Oral Step, including meeting to discuss the grievance if such meeting is requested by the employee or the employee's representative or if a meeting is deemed necessary by the Oral Step representative. The Oral Step representative shall communicate a decision to the employee and the employee's representative, if any, within fourteen (14) days following the date the grievance is received at the Oral Step.

ii. If the employee elects not to utilize the oral discussion provision of this Section, he may file a formal grievance at Step 1, provided such written grievance is filed within fourteen (14) days following the occurrence of the event giving rise to the grievance.

iii. Failure to communicate the decision within the specified time limit shall permit the employee, or the Union where appropriate, to proceed to the next step.

iv. The number of days indicated at this Step shall be considered as the maximum, and every effort will be made to expedite the process. However, the time limits specified in any step of this procedure may be extended in writing in any specific instance as long as necessary provided there is mutual agreement by both sides.

b. <u>Step 1</u>

i. In filing a grievance at Step 1, the employee or the designated

---

employee representative shall submit to the Step 1 Management Representative a grievance form furnished by the Union setting forth specifically the complete facts on which the grievance is based, the specific provision or provisions of the Agreement allegedly violated, and the relief requested. All written documents to be considered by the Step 1 Management Representative shall be submitted with the grievance form; however, if additional written documentation is obtained after the grievance is filed, such documentation may be presented at the Step 1 meeting.

ii. The Step 1 Management Representative or his designated representative shall have a meeting to discuss the grievance and shall communicate a decision in writing to the employee and the employee's representative, if any, within fourteen (14) days following the date the grievance is received at Step 1.

iii. Failure to communicate the decision within the specified time limit shall permit the employee, or the Union where appropriate, to proceed to the next step.

iv. The number of days indicated at

this Step shall be considered as the maximum, and every effort will be made to expedite the process. However, the time limits specified in any step of this procedure may be extended in writing in any specific instance as long as necessary provided there is mutual agreement by both sides.

c. Step 2

    i. If the grievance is not resolved at Step 1, the employee or the employee's representative may submit it in writing to the Department Manager or his designated representative within fourteen (14) days after receipt of the decision at Step 1. The grievance shall include a copy of the grievance form submitted at Step 1 and a copy of the Step 1 response, together with all written documents in support of the grievance. When the grievance is eligible for initiation at Step 2, the grievance form must contain the same information as a grievance filed at Step 1 above.

    ii. The Department Manager or his designated representative may have a meeting with the employee and/or the designated Union Staff Representative to discuss the grievance. The Plant Manager or his designated representative shall communicate a decision in writing within twenty-one (21) days following receipt of the written grievance.

iii. Failure to communicate the decision within the specified time limit shall permit the employee, or the Union where appropriate, to proceed to the next step.

iv. The number of days indicated at this step shall be considered as the maximum, and every effort will be made to expedite the process. However, the time limits specified in any step of this procedure may be extended in writing in any specific instance as long as necessary provided there is mutual agreement by both sides.

d. Step 3

i. If the grievance is not resolved at Step 2, the designated Union representative, or the employee if not represented by the Union, may appeal the Step 2 decision, in writing, to the Department of Human Resources within fourteen (14) days after receipt of the decision at Step 2. The grievance shall include a copy of the grievance form submitted at Steps 1 and 2, together with all written responses and documents in support of the grievance. The Department of Management Services may have a meeting with the Union President or the designated Union representative to discuss the grievance. When the grievance is eligible for initiation at Step 3, the grievance form must contain the same information as the grievance filed at Step 1 above.

ii. The Department of Human Resources shall communicate a decision in writing to the employee and the Union President or the designated Union representative within twenty-one (21) days following receipt of the written grievance.

iii. Failure to communicate the decision within the specified time limit shall permit the employee, or the Union where appropriate, to proceed to the next step.

iv. The number of days indicated at this step shall be considered as the maximum, and every effort will be made to expedite the process. However, the time limits specified in any step of this procedure may be extended in writing in any specific instance as long as necessary provided there is mutual agreement by both sides.

SECTION 4 - Time Limits

(A)   Failure to initiate or appeal a grievance within the time limits specified shall be deemed a waiver of the grievance.

(B)   Failure at any step of this procedure to communicate the decision on a grievance within the specified time limit shall permit the employee, or the Union where appropriate, to proceed to the next step. A Step 2 or Step 3 answer that is not received by the Union by the written, agreed-to deadline does not alter the time limits for appealing a grievance to the next step.

(C)   Claims of either an untimely filing or untimely appeal shall be made at the step-in question.

SECTION 5 - Exceptions

(A)   Nothing in this Article or elsewhere in this Agreement shall be construed to permit the Union or an employee to process a grievance: (1) on behalf of any employee without his consent, or (2) when the subject of such (employee's) grievance, is at the same time the subject of an administrative action, or appeal before a governmental board or agency, or court proceeding.

(B)   All grievances will be presented at the Oral Step, with the following exceptions:

        a.   If a grievance arises from the action of an official higher than the Step 1 Management Representative, the grievance shall be initiated at Step 2 or 3 as appropriate, by submitting a grievance form as set forth in Step 1 within fourteen (14) days following the occurrence of the event giving rise to the grievance.

    b. The Union shall have the right to bring a class action grievance on behalf of bargaining Unit employees in its own name, concerning disputes relating to the interpretation or application of this Agreement. Such grievance shall not include disciplinary actions taken against any employee. The Union's election to proceed under this Article shall preclude it from proceeding in another forum on the same issue. The class action grievance shall identify the employees adversely impacted by the dispute relating to the interpretation or application of the Agreement. Such grievance shall be initiated at Step 2 of this procedure, in accordance with the provisions set forth herein, within fourteen (14) days of the occurrence of the event giving rise to the grievance.

(C)   Any employee who has not attained permanent status can only bring non-discipline grievances to Step 3 as provided for in this Article.

GRIEVANCE (version 5)

Section 1. To promote better Employer/employee relationship, both parties pledge their immediate cooperation to settle any grievances or complaints that might arise out of and in the course of employment with the Employer, and the following procedure shall be the sole procedure to be utilized for that purpose.

Section 2. Disciplinary actions or measures shall include reprimand, demotion, suspension and discharge. Disciplinary action or measures may be imposed only for just cause. Any disciplinary action or measure imposed upon an employee may be processed as a grievance through the regular grievance procedure. If the Employer has reason to reprimand an employee, every effort will be made not to embarrass the employee before other employees or the public. If the Employer has reason to discuss any disciplinary action, the employee shall be given the option of having a Union representative present at any such discussion.

The Employer shall not discharge any employee who has completed the introductory period without just cause. If the Employer feels that there is just cause for discharge, the employee involved will be suspended without pay for seven (7) calendar days before the discharge is effective. The employee and the Union representative will be notified in writing that the employee has been suspended and is subject to discharge. Such notification shall state the nature of the offense for which the employee is being discharged, in detail, specifying dates, locations and the particular nature of the offense committed by the employee. The Union shall have the right to appeal any disciplinary action within seven (7) calendar days of receipt of notice as a grievance at Section 4 of the grievance procedure.

Section 3. Any employee claiming a breach of any provision of this Agreement shall refer the matter to the appropriate Supervisor within five (5) working days of the date upon which the alleged violation occurred. The employee may be accompanied by a Union representative in any discussion following such reference to the Supervisor. The Union may take up any alleged violation of this Agreement, with or without permission of the employee.

Section 4. If the matter is not settled within five (5) working days of the reference to the appropriate Supervisor, the matter may be referred to the Operations Manager, provided that such reference shall be in writing, shall state the nature of the grievance, the section of the contract allegedly violated, and the remedy requested and shall be presented within ten (10) working days of the expiration of the five (5) day period for settlement with the Supervisor. The Operations Manager, or designee, and such assistants as the manager may select shall meet promptly to settle such grievance with the grievance committee.

Section 5. Should the grievance committee and the Operations Manager fail to effect a settlement of the dispute within ten (10) days of its submission to the Operations Manager, the Union shall have the right to submit the grievance in writing to the Senior Manager, or designee, provided that such submission shall be within twenty (20) days from the date of submission to the Operations Manager as provided for above.

Section 6. Should the parties fail to settle the dispute with the Senior within two (2) weeks from the date of submission to the Senior Manager, the Union shall have the right to submit the matter to arbitration in accordance with the procedures outlined in Article ____.

Discipline

Disciplinary action in labor agreements usually begins with a provision regarding "just cause." The vast majority of labor contracts will only allow the termination of non-probationary union members or individuals for just cause. This can either be dealt with in a grievance procedure or arbitration provision or in a separate provision on disciplinary action.

The reason not all contracts contain a disciplinary action provision because some companies treat disciplinary action as a management right. These companies reserve the right to make all disciplinary decisions with perhaps a statement that they agree that discipline will only be for just cause. Other companies will include a listing of work rules or infractions that can result in disciplinary action. This is a compromise for employers whose unions do not wish to give the employer broad authority under its management rights clause to discipline numbers.

In addition some disciplinary action provisions relate more to how disciplinary warnings will be treated for a particular bargaining unit member. For example, some provisions will limit the length of time that a particular disciplinary warning can stay in an individual's personnel file or how long it can be used as evidence of rules infractions or to compound later disciplinary action.

Below you will find a couple of examples of disciplinary action contract provisions. The first clause provides for removal of disciplinary action warnings after a 9-month period. There is an exception made for disciplinary action that is documented and succeeded by additional disciplinary action during the nine months. A suspension or termination letter becomes a permanent part of the employee's file. The provision also provides that the employee has the right to review his or her personnel file at any time.

The second version gives the company a broad right for disciplinary action but makes that subject to the grievance procedure for non-probationary employees. It specifically states that oral counseling is not subject to the grievance procedure, but it also cannot be used as part of any future disciplinary action if it is older than 12 months old. Written reprimands, on the other hand, may be grieved but they are limited to Step 3 and are removed from the personnel file after 18 months. All other discipline including reduction in base pay, demotion, suspension or termination begins the grievance proceeding at Step 2 and can then be appealed to arbitration.

This clause is somewhat unique in that it also provides for specific requirements for due process in the investigation of disciplinary matters. This clause seems to me to cut two ways; if the employer follows the due process listed in the provision it should feel good about its chances of prevailing at arbitration; on the other hand, any misstep during the investigation process is outlined in the provision would provide a perfect opportunity for an arbitrator to overturn a disciplinary decision. Overall, I would attempt to reach a disciplinary action compromise without including specific procedural steps that discipline would go through.

DISCIPLINE (version 1)

Warning and discipline letters may be removed from the employee's official file following a period of nine months after the date of the letter, unless a succeeding letter covering the same offence has been placed into the file within the nine month period. All letters, which impose a suspension or termination, must remain a permanent part of the employee's official file. Employees may review their official personnel file at any time.

DISCIPLINE (version 2)
SECTION 1 - Disciplinary Action

(A)   Reductions in base pay, demotions, suspensions, and dismissals may be affected by the Company at any time against any employee. Such actions against employees with permanent status shall be grievable in accordance with the grievance procedure in Article 6, if the employee alleges that the action was not for just cause. Demotion will not be used as a form of disciplinary action for employees in the classes of [List Job Classifications]. Disciplinary actions shall be subject to the grievance procedure as follows:

   (1)   Oral reprimands shall not be grievable under the provisions of this Agreement.

   (2)   An oral reprimand will not be considered in determining progressive discipline provided the employee is not disciplined for the same offense during the succeeding twelve (12) months.

   (3)   Written reprimands may be grieved up to Step 3 and the decision at that level

shall be final and binding.

(4)   A written reprimand will not be considered in determining progressive discipline provided the employee is not disciplined for the same offense during the succeeding eighteen (18) months, and the written reprimand was not for a major offense which could have resulted in the employee's dismissal.

(B)   A complaint by an employee with permanent status concerning any written reprimand which contains criminal allegations or criminal charges, may be grieved through the arbitration step of the grievance procedure.

(C)   If filed within fourteen (14) calendar days from the date of receipt of notice from the Company, by personal delivery or by certified mail, return receipt requested, a complaint by an employee with permanent status concerning a reduction in base pay, suspension, demotion, or dismissal may be grieved at Step 2 and processed through the Arbitration Step, in accordance with the Grievance Procedure in Article 6 of this Agreement.

SECTION 2 - Disciplinary Investigations. In the course of any disciplinary investigation, the investigation methods employed will be consistent with this Article.

(A)   Definitions: For the purpose of this section the following definitions of terms shall apply:

    a.   "Disciplinary Investigation" refers to an investigation meeting with respect to an incident or complaint between a member of management or supervision, including an investigator, and an employee covered by this Agreement in which the information to be obtained at the investigation meeting will be the basis for the decision as to whether to suspend or dismiss the employee. It does not include counseling sessions, or investigations, which may result in lesser forms of disciplinary action or meetings at which the employee is solely being advised of intended disciplinary action, and offered an opportunity to explain why he should not be disciplined.

    b. "Complainants" refers to the complaining or charging party relative to an incident or complaint.

(B)   Procedures

    a. Whenever an employee covered by this Agreement is under investigation and subject to interview by members of management for any reason, which could lead to disciplinary action, suspension, demotion, or dismissal, such interview shall be conducted under the following conditions:

        i. The interview shall be conducted at a reasonable hour, preferably at a time when the employee is on duty, unless the seriousness of the investigation is of such a degree that immediate action is required.

        ii. The employee under investigation shall be informed of the manager in charge of the investigation and all persons present during the interview.

iii. The employee under investigation shall be informed of the nature of the investigation prior to any interview, and he shall be informed of the name of all complainants.

iv. At the request of any employee under investigation, he shall have the right to be represented by his Union steward or other designee, who shall be present at all times during such interview.

v. Where the Company determines that a complaint is unsupported by the facts or is otherwise without merit, or determines that the facts are insufficient to discipline the employee under investigation, such conclusion will be so noted as part of the investigative record. Written documents relative to the investigation are subject to the provisions of Article 12, Personnel Records.

vi. Where the employee is the subject of the investigation, the employee shall be provided the opportunity to review all written statements made by the complainant and witnesses immediately prior to the beginning of the investigation interview.

(C) Unless required by statute, no employee shall be

required to submit to a polygraph test or any device designed to measure the truthfulness of his response during an investigation of a complaint or allegation. If an employee is offered an opportunity to submit to a polygraph test, the employee's refusal will not be referred to in any final action taken by the Company.

(D)   Alleged violations of the investigative rights provided for in this section by an employee or the Union shall be investigated by the Company. The Company shall provide the employee and the Union with an explanation concerning the alleged violation and corrective action taken, if any.

(E)   The Company will make a good faith effort to complete all internal investigations within sixty (60) days from the date the investigation is assigned to the investigator. Except in the case of a criminal investigation, the employee shall be notified in writing of any investigation that exceeds one hundred and twenty (120) calendar days. The employee under investigation shall be advised of the results of the investigation at its conclusion.

(F)   The provisions of this section may be grieved in accordance with Article 6, up to and including Step 3 of the Grievance Procedure whose decision shall be final and binding.

(G)   In cases where the Company determines that the employee's absence from the work location is essential to the investigation and the employee cannot be reassigned to other duties pending completion of the investigation, the employee shall be placed on administrative leave. In cases where the employee can be reassigned, the reassigned employee may be offered the option to return to the original work location if the charges or allegations against him are not sustained.

Section 3. Employee Copy. Each employee shall be furnished a copy of all disciplinary entries placed in his official personnel file and shall be permitted to respond thereto, and a copy of the employee's response shall be placed in the employee's personnel file.

Personnel Records
Labor contracts will sometimes include provisions regarding personnel records. These clauses are not as common in labor contracts as they are in non-union employee handbooks. When included in labor contracts they usually deal with two issues: when these records can be reviewed by employees and how long information that is included in the personnel records will remain active or even physically in the personnel file.

These clauses should be read in relation to grievance procedures or disciplinary action clauses. They normally limit in some way the employer's right to use the personnel record against the employee. In some cases they also protect the employer; a company may wish to include a provision like this in order to clarify its right to include or exclude certain information from personnel files to comply with HIPPA, ADA, FMLA, or other state and federal requirements.

Clause Summary and Drafting Notes
There is one model clause included. It states there is only one official personnel file but allows for duplicate records in departments. It states that all derogatory information will be copied to employees who will have a right to review and respond to information in the personnel file. It further gives the right to the employee to review and copy his personnel file documents. It states that letters of counseling and other disciplinary action will remain active for only 12 months but will remain part of the personnel file indefinitely to serve as proof of prior notice in future discipline cases. This clause is relatively neutral.

PERSONNEL RECORDS (version 1)
Section 1. Personnel Files.
(A)   There shall be only one official personnel file for each employee, which shall be maintained in the central personnel office of the employing Company unless a different location is designated by the Director of Human Resources or its designee. Duplicate personnel files may be established and maintained within a Department. Such duplicate personnel files may contain part, or all of the items filed in the official personnel file but may not contain any items that are not filed in the official personnel file. Information in an employee's official personnel file shall only refer to matters concerning (affecting) the employee's job or related to his Company employment.

(B)   If any derogatory material is placed in an employee's official personnel file, a copy will be sent to the employee. The employee will have the right to answer any such material filed, and his answer will be attached to the file copy.

(C)   An employee will have the right to review his own official personnel file and any duplicate personnel files at reasonable times under the supervision of the designated records custodian.

(D)   Where the Plant Manager or its designee, the courts, an arbitrator, or other statutory authority determines that a document has been placed in the employee's personnel file in error or is otherwise invalid, such document shall be placed in an envelope together with a letter of explanation. The envelope shall be sealed, stamped "NOT VALID", and retained in the employee's personnel file for at least one (1) year after final action; provided, however, that the document shall be removed upon the employee's written request in accordance with the foregoing records schedule.

Section 2. Letters of Counseling.

(A)   The Company and the Union agree that a letter of counseling or counseling notice is not discipline and not subject to the grievance procedure. Such materials are documentation of minor work deficiencies and are appropriately utilized in evaluating the performance of an employee or documenting adherence to the Company's standards of conduct.

(B)   A letter of counseling or counseling notice will not be considered in determining progressive discipline provided the employee has not been counseled or disciplined for the same offense during the succeeding twelve (12) months, except it may be cited to demonstrate the employee had been previously noticed of the same performance or conduct deficiency.

Performance Evaluations

This is another unique clause I ran across while researching the book, although it is not very common in unionized environments. The purpose of this clause is to clarify management's authority to give employees performance evaluations as well as to state under what cases these performance evaluations may be used for discipline and under what cases they can be subject to the grievance procedure. The basic issues in this compromise are management's right to evaluate and demand performance at a certain level against the union's interest in protecting members from unjust or unfair disciplinary action.

Clause Summary and Drafting Notes

This clause gives management the right to evaluate employees and states that the performance evaluation will not be subject to the grievance procedure unless the evaluation itself serves as a basis for a disciplinary suspension or dismissal. It states that employees will be given a reasonable opportunity to correct performance deficiencies and states that the performance evaluation process, whether good or bad, does not preclude management from disciplining employees for violations of specific standards. Overall this seems a reasonable middle ground; management can judge and discipline for poor performance, subject to the grievance machinery at the last stages of discipline.

PERFORMANCE EVALUATIONS (version 1)

(A)   Employees shall be evaluated by their immediate supervisors or designated raters, who shall be held accountable for such reviews.

(B)   The Parties agree that performance evaluations are not grievable; however a performance evaluation may be contested if it serves as the basis for a suspension or dismissal.

(C)   Any employee who has attained permanent status in his current class or occupational level for a position shall be provided a reasonable opportunity to correct performance deficiencies.

(D)   The use of counseling shall not preclude the Company from seeking to discipline an employee for cause based upon a specific violation of a conduct standard.

Arbitration

Like the grievance procedure articles discussed earlier, arbitration clauses are among the most critical in any labor/management compromise. These clauses define the authority of arbitrators and the procedures that arbitrators must follow in deciding disputes between labor and management. These clauses must be read in conjunction with the grievance procedures found in their respective agreements.

Like the grievance and discipline compromises, there are several key interests at stake between management and the union in reaching the arbitration compromise:

- ❑ How much of that management rights authority the company is willing to cede to the arbitrator?
- ❑ Who arbitrates the claims? How is their neutrality assured?
- ❑ What can be arbitrated? What issues are the parties willing to leave in the hands of an outsider? What complaints are outside the jurisdiction of the arbitrator?
- ❑ What remedies are available to (or removed from) the arbitrator?
- ❑ What procedures must be followed to ensure due process and fairness?

Clause Summaries and Drafting Notes

Arbitration provisions typically outline the following key issues:

Procedure for choosing the arbitrator(s)
The company and union will typically agree to have one or more of the arbitrators chosen from a list provided by either the American Arbitration Association or the

Federal Mediation and Conciliation Service. In addition, sometimes the arbitration panel will include one or more members appointed by each of the parties without the approval of the other parties.

In other circumstances the panel is a standing panel agreed to in advance by the company and the union. In rare cases the grievance procedure will give the final authority to resolve grievances to a member of the company. This is not the normal situation; typically, employees expect to receive representation from the union and a hearing from a neutral third party to ultimately resolve grievances. However, this is an option and, in some cases, an acceptable compromise.

The jurisdiction of the arbitrator.
Often the parties will compromise over what areas they will give the arbitrator latitude to decide. Clauses will sometimes prohibit an arbitrator from providing relief for something that is not specifically provided for in the terms of the labor agreement. Parties will often prohibit an arbitrator from providing back pay or other remedies for a time period prior to the date of the filing of the grievance. Many contracts also prohibit an arbitrator from hearing the case that occurs after the expiration of the collective bargaining agreement. These clauses are written to provide more certainties to the parties about subjects or remedies on which an arbitrator may act. The most common way to limit an arbitrator's jurisdiction is to limit the contract provisions an arbitrator is allowed to review. There are several examples of clauses in this book that specifically say that the clause is not subject to the grievance and arbitration procedure, making it off-limits to the

arbitrator.

The time limits for arbitration

Most grievance clauses prohibit grievances from being
processed if filed long after the event giving rise to the
complaint. Parties will often prohibit an arbitrator
from providing back pay or other remedies for a time
period prior to the date of the filing of the grievance.
Many contracts also prohibit an arbitrator from hearing
the case that occurs after the expiration of the collective
bargaining agreement.

How the expenses for arbitration will be borne

Most arbitration clauses also outline how the parties
will pay the arbitrator(s). Usually expenses for the
arbitrator are shared by the parties, although some
clauses provide a "loser pays" system, in essence
penalizing the losing party for not settling the case
before arbitration. This is a way to limit "frivolous"
arbitration cases (although even if the expenses are
shared arbitration cases today are still expensive).

Limitations on remedies available

As discussed earlier, many clauses limit the remedies
available to an arbitrator, or limit the length of time for
which an arbitrator is allowed to provide a remedy.

Appeal rights, if any

Most arbitration decisions are final and ineligible for
appeal except in extreme cases, like when the arbitrator
issues an award for a complaint specifically outside the
arbitrator's authority.

There are five model versions of arbitration clauses that

follow. The first clause selects arbitrators through the Federal Mediation and Conciliation Service (FMCS) panel using an alternate strike procedure. Each party bears its own expenses, but the loser pays the fees of the arbitrator. It extinguishes the right to arbitrate claims that occur after the collective bargaining agreement expires, and prohibits remedies that are retroactive beyond the date of which the company is presented with the "difference" by the union. As a note on drafting, I would clearly define "difference" (maybe just limit the remedy to the date on which the grievance is filed, or a short time before that date certain). A smart union attorney attempting to win a large back-pay award could certainly define the word "difference" much more broadly and expansively than simply the date on which the company received the initial grievance. This provides much more leeway than most companies should be comfortable with.

The second version gives the parties a short period of time (10 days) to request an arbitration panel. The panel is chosen in a unique way: the company and the union each pick their own representative and those two panelists choose the third panel member who will act as the Chairman. Where the company and union panelists cannot agree they are required to choose a panel member from the American Arbitration Association (AAA). I have recently had some negative experience with AAA and would not recommend using them for labor arbitration panels (they are increasingly interested in forcing you to follow THEIR rules, instead of enforcing YOUR agreement). Nevertheless, that is the service negotiated in this clause. There is some language restricting the authority of the arbitrators (they cannot modify the agreement). Each party bears the expense of its own panel member and they share the expenses of the third member whether they win or lose the arbitration case. It also states that there can be No-Lockout or strike during the term of any arbitration case. This is an interesting clause and seems relatively neutral. It does not clearly limit remedies as well as the first model clause.

The third version also has a 10-day period in which to appeal. It also uses the one panelist chosen by each side with the third panelist chosen from an FMCS list, who acts as the chairperson. Expenses are shared equally except for each party's own witnesses or representatives. The clause also limits the scope of the arbitration and limits the use of past practice. This is another good "compromise" clause.

The fourth clause is an excellent example of an attempt by the company to strictly limit the authority of the arbitrator. It specifically limits both the jurisdiction of the arbitrator as well as the authority to make awards. It is a solid clause for management and a good place to start when drafting limited arbitration language.

The fifth clause is relatively brief and open-ended. It has one section stating limiting the arbitrator's authority, but the limitations are somewhat broad. There is virtually no limit to remedy, so long as the award does not "alter, modify, amend, add to or detract from" the contract. The remedy can go back 60 days from the date the grievance is filed. This is a clause most favorable to the union member bringing the grievance.

ARBITRATION (version 1)

Section 1. Disputes involving the interpretation or application of the provisions of this Agreement are subject to arbitration. Matters involving employee grievances shall be brought to formal arbitration only after attempts to resolve the grievance in the steps as outlined in the Grievance Procedure are completed.

Section 2. When the Union invokes the arbitration procedure, the Union will request a panel of arbitrators from the Federal Mediation and Conciliation Service. The FMCS shall send the list of arbitrators to the authorized representatives of the Union and the Company. The arbitrator will be selected from the panel by the parties, alternately striking a name until a single arbitrator is selected. The party to strike the first name shall be determined by the toss of a coin. Either party reserves the right to reject only one list from the FMCS and request another list prior to striking of names. The Arbitrator shall conduct a hearing as expeditiously as is possible and shall render his decision promptly and without undue delay. The decision of the Arbitrator shall be final and binding on both parties.

Section 3. In the course of hearings before the arbitrator, the Company and the Union shall be afforded a full opportunity to present any evidence, written or oral, which may be pertinent to the matter before the arbitrator.

Section 4. Each party shall bear their own expenses. The fees of the arbitrator shall be borne by the losing party. The arbitrator shall only interpret the Agreement and shall not modify, amend, add to or delete from any of its provisions in deciding the issue(s) submitted to him by the parties as contained in the above grievance procedure.

Section 5. Employees covered by this Agreement cannot, except through the duly constituted officials of the Union, initiate the arbitration procedures set forth in this Article.

Section 6. No arbitration award shall grant relief extending beyond the termination date of this contract, nor be retroactive beyond the date upon which the difference was first presented to the Company.

ARBITRATION (version 2)

Section 1. If a grievance is not settled by the final step of the grievance procedure outlined in Article ___ and it involves the interpretation, application, or claimed violation of any provision of this agreement, then either party may, upon written demand given to the other party, within ten (10) working days (after the Company's answer in the last step or the Union's answer to the Company's claim of violation of the no-strike pledge), submit said dispute or grievance to arbitration, as follows.

Section 2. The arbitration shall proceed before a Board of Arbitration, which shall consist of three members. One member shall be appointed by the Company, one member by the Union and the two members so appointed, shall select the third member, who shall act as chairman of the board. Within five (5) working days after the written demand for arbitration is made as above provided, the party demanding arbitration shall notify the other party, in writing, of the person appointed as its member of the Board of Arbitration. Within five (5) working days after receipt of said notice of appointment the other party shall likewise notify, in writing, the person appointed as its member. Within five (5) working days thereafter the two persons so appointed shall select the third member to act as chairman of the board.

Section 3. If either party or their appointed members fail or refuse, within the aforesaid time, to make the appointment or selection, as aforesaid, then either party may, upon written notice to the other, request the American Arbitration Association to make said appointment or selection, as the case may be according to its rules or to fill any vacancies that may occur that the parties fail or refuse to fill. The arbitration proceeding shall be conducted under the rules of the American Arbitration Association, whose rules are incorporated by reference. The Board of Arbitration shall not have authority to add to, subtract from, modify, change, or alter any of the provisions of this agreement. The Board shall decide the dispute and render its award by majority vote; and the Board's award shall be final and binding on the parties. Each party shall bear the expenses of its appointed member, representatives, and witnesses; and the fees and expenses of the Board's chairman shall be home equally by the parties.

Section 4. Pending the processing of the grievance and the award of the Board of Arbitration and during the term of this agreement there shall be no stoppage, slowdown, or other interference with work in accordance with No-Strike, No Lock-Out Provision of this agreement.

ARBITRATION (version 3)
Section 1. If the grievance is not settled in the Grievance Procedure outlined in Article ___, the Local Union Executive Board may present the grievance to

the Director of Labor Relations for arbitration within 10 workdays after receipt of the Director of Labor Relations Step 4 response.

Section 2. The arbitration panel shall be composed of 1 representative appointed by the Director of Labor Relations, one representative appointed by the Union and a third member chosen by the two appointed representatives from a list provided by the Federal Mediation Conciliation Service. The member chosen by the two representatives shall serve as Chairman of the panel. A decision approved by any two members of the panel shall be binding on the parties. The cost of services of the Chairman of the panel, court reporter, transcripts and all other costs incurred by the panel, except compensation of the two original appointees, shall be borne equally by both parties. Neither side shall be responsible for the expense of the other's witnesses or representatives.

Section 3. The scope of the arbitration is limited to the terms of this Agreement and any supplemental agreements between the parties. The arbitrators shall have no authority to amend, modify, nullify, ignore, add to, or subtract from the provisions of this Agreement. The arbitrators shall only consider and make a decision with respect to the particular issues necessary to resolve the grievance without recommendation or comment on any other matter. The arbitrators shall be without power to make a decision or render an award contrary to or inconsistent with or modifying or varying in any way the application of laws, rules, and regulations having the force and effect of law. No liability shall accrue against the Employer for a date prior to the date the grievance was presented in Step 1. The arbitrators shall submit in writing their decision and award within 30 calendar days following the close of the hearing or the submission of briefs by the parties, whichever is later. The decision and award shall be based solely upon the arbitrator's interpretation of the meaning or application to the facts of this Agreement to the grievance presented. Past practices may be considered in interpreting an ambiguous provision of this Agreement but may not be considered for the purpose of creating an employee right for Employer obligation or liability. Subject to the provisions of this section, the decision of the arbitrators shall be binding on the parties.

ARBITRATION (version 4)
Section 1. If the grievance is not resolved at Step 3, the President of the Union, or a designated member of his staff, may appeal the Step 3 decision to Arbitration on a Request for Arbitration Form (to be supplied by the Company) within fourteen (14) days after receipt of the decision at Step 3.

Section 2. The parties agree to the following procedures for any arbitration cases heard under this Article:

(A)   The parties may, by mutual agreement in writing, submit related grievances for hearing before the same arbitrator.

(B)   The arbitrator shall be one person from a panel of five (5) permanent arbitrators, mutually selected by the Company and the Union to serve in rotation for any case or cases submitted.

(C)   Arbitration hearings shall be held at times and locations mutually agreed to by the parties, taking into consideration the availability of evidence, location of witnesses, existence of appropriate facilities, and other relevant factors. If mutual agreement cannot be reached, the arbitration hearing shall be held in [City Name].

(D)   The arbitrator may fashion an appropriate remedy to resolve the grievance and, provided the decision is in accordance with his jurisdiction and authority under this Agreement, shall be final and binding on the Company, the Union, the grievant(s), and the employees in the bargaining unit. In considering a grievance the arbitrator shall be governed by the following provisions and limitations:

    a. The arbitrator shall issue his decision not later than thirty (30) days from the date of the closing of the hearing or the submission of briefs, whichever is later.

    b. The arbitrator's decision shall be in writing, and shall set forth the arbitrator's opinion and conclusions on the precise issue(s) submitted.

    c. The arbitrator shall have no authority to determine any other issue, and the arbitrator shall refrain from issuing any statement of opinion or conclusion not essential to the determination of the issues submitted.

    d. The arbitrator shall limit his decision strictly to the application and interpretation of the specific provisions of this Agreement.

Section 3. The arbitrator shall be without power or authority to make any decisions:

    (A)   Contrary to or inconsistent with, adding

to, subtracting from, or modifying, altering or ignoring in any way, the terms of this Agreement, or of applicable law or rules or regulations having the force and effect of law; or

(B) Limiting or interfering in any way with the powers, duties and responsibilities of the Company, applicable law, and rules and regulations having the force and effect of law, except as such powers, duties and responsibilities have been abridged, delegated or modified by the expressed provisions of this Agreement; or

(C) Which has the effect of restricting the discretion of the Company as otherwise granted by law unless such authority is modified by this Agreement; or

(D) That is based solely upon Company past practice or policy unless such agency practice or policy is contrary to law or this Agreement.

Section 4. The arbitrator's award may include back pay to the grievant(s); however, the following limitations shall apply to such monetary awards:

(A) No award for back pay shall exceed the amount of pay the employee would otherwise have earned at his regular rate of pay and such back pay shall not be retroactive to a date earlier than the date of the occurrence of the event giving rise to the grievance under consideration and in no event more than the time limits permitted for initiation of the grievance.

(B) The award shall not exceed the actual loss to the

grievant and will not include punitive damages.

(C) The fees and expenses of the arbitrator shall be borne solely by the party who fails to prevail in the hearing; however, each party shall be responsible for compensating and paying the expenses of its own representatives, attorneys and witnesses. Should the arbitrator fashion an award in such a manner that the grievance is sustained in part and denied in part, the Company and Union will evenly split the arbitrator's fee and expenses.

(A) The Union will not be responsible for costs of an arbitration to which it was not a party.

ARBITRATION (version 5)

Section 1. In the event the Union elects to appeal a grievance to arbitration under this Agreement, it must notify the Labor Relations Manager of its decision in writing within twenty-one (21) calendar days from the date upon which the grievance was submitted to the Senior Manager. After the grievance has been so submitted, the parties or their representatives shall jointly request the Federal Mediation and Conciliation Service for a list of seven (7) arbitrators. The parties shall select an arbitrator from that list by such method as they may jointly select or, if they are unable to agree upon a method, then by the method of alternate striking of names under which the grieving party shall strike the first name objectionable to it, and the Employer shall then strike the first name objectionable to it. The final name left on the list shall be the arbitrator. The parties shall have ten (10) working days to set the hearing as provided by dates available to the arbitrator.

Section 2. The arbitrator's decision shall be final and binding, but the arbitrator shall have no power to alter, modify, amend, add to or detract from the terms of this Agreement. The arbitrator's decision shall be within the scope and terms of this Agreement and in writing.

Section 3. The arbitrator may also provide retroactivity not exceeding sixty (60) days prior to the date the grievance is filed and shall state the effective date.

Section 4. Failure of either party to meet the time requirements set forth shall be deemed to have defaulted the grievance unless both parties mutually agree in writing to extend the time limits provided. The Employer and the Unions shall divide equally and pay the arbitrator's fee, the cost of any hearing room and cost of a court reporter if requested by the arbitrator. All other expenses shall be paid by the party incurring them.

No-Strike No-Lockout

The No-Strike/No-Lockout clause (along with management rights, union security and a grievance/arbitration procedure) is among the most common compromises in all labor agreements. The No-Strike/No-Lockout compromise is typically exchanged together. The purpose of the compromise should be obvious: to gain labor peace during the term of the collective bargaining agreement.

Clause Summaries and Drafting Notes

The key aspects to a No-Strike/No Lockout clause for both sides is to make the provision as ironclad as possible. Typically, the No-Strike provision will include significantly more verbiage, usually surrounding what the union will do to prevent its members from engaging in an unauthorized or "wildcat" strike or other work stoppage. In addition, the no-strike provision will also contain as broad a definition of strike as the union is willing to decree, including any type of work slowdown or other kind of stoppage. Further, the no-strike and no-lockout pledges will also typically include a description of the type of damages that either party agrees to pay if they should violate the pledge and the agreement.

Because this compromise is so common, there are six model No-Strike/No-Lockout clauses included below. The first version contains a very strong No-Strike pledge stating that strikes are prohibited no matter what causes them, including things that were not in the contemplation of the parties at the time of negotiations. This is about as broad No-Strike pledge as you can get. It gives the company authority for immediate termination of employees not subject to the grievance procedure for violation of the pledge, including the leadership of the union. It also states that there will not be a lockout. It provides an expedited arbitration procedure to determine if the clause is violated and awards the injunctive relief and damages in federal court for violations. This clause is a good one, especially for management (although the remedies work both directions). The No-Strike pledge is about as ironclad as they come.

The second version contains the No-Strike pledge and includes language regarding slowdowns or other kinds of stoppages or other interference of the company's operation. This language is not as strong as the first clause in terms of the causes of the strike, but is a little stronger in terms of the breadth of what is included. It also has a No-Lockout pledge. It says that it applies to disputes outside of the company (i.e. sympathy strikes). Finally, it gives the company the right to terminate employees for violation of the pledge.

The third version contains a No-Lockout pledge but states that a plant may close, or an operation may shut down for business reasons without being considered a lockout. This is excellent language for the company. The No-Strike pledge is very broad, including a sit down, slow down, stoppage, picket, boycott or other disturbances. This is an excellent and broad description of items that can be considered outside of the bounds of the typical No-Strike pledge. It states that employees who violate the No-Strike clause are subject to disciplinary action and termination. It states that the union will make affirmative actions to stop a strike in violation of the agreement and a failure to do so is considered leading and instigating the strike. This is a way the company can hold the union leadership responsible for the actions of its members.

The fourth version of the No-Strike pledge is very simple stating that there is No-Lockout or strike. It broadly defines strikes to include sit-down strikes, slowdowns, walk-outs or any other impeding of the operations. This is a good, basic clause, although it may not protect the company from some of the more nuanced issues in the more detailed clauses above (sympathy, informational picket).

The fifth version is also very simple and defines a strike as a slowdown or interruption and states that there will be No-Lockout. This clause is perhaps too simple and does not provide as much protection for the company as the first three model clauses.

The sixth version is unique in that it does not include a No-Lockout pledge by the company; this is very uncommon, and obviously to the advantage of the company. It includes language on the union and its agents. It broadly defines the strike to include interference with the company's operations. It contains affirmative obligations for the union to notify members, officers and other representatives of their obligations under the contract and gives the company the right to terminate employees outside of the grievance procedure, violation of the No-Strike pledge. Finally, it gives the company a right to go court to enforce the No-Strike pledge.

NO-STRIKE/NO-LOCKOUT (with Binding Arbitration) (version 1)

Section 1. No-Strikes. In consideration of the Company's commitment as set forth in Section 3 of this Article, the Union, its officers, agents, representatives, stewards, committeemen and members, and all other employees shall not, in any way, directly or indirectly, instigate, lead, engage in, authorize, cause, assist, encourage, participate in, ratify, or condone any strike, sympathy strike, slowdown, work stoppage, or any other interference with or interruption of work at any of the Company's operations, whether or not such a strike, sympathy strike, slowdown, work stoppage, or other interference with or interruption of work (a) involves a matter subject to resolution pursuant to the grievance and arbitration procedures set forth in Article ___ of this Agreement; or (b) involves a matter specifically referred to or covered in this Agreement; or (c) involves a matter which has been discussed between the Company and the Union; or (d) involves a matter which was not within the knowledge or the contemplation of the Company and the Union at the time this Agreement was negotiated or executed.

Section 2. Discipline. The failure or refusal on the part of any employee to comply with the provisions of Section 1 of this Article shall be cause for immediate discipline, including discharge, and such discipline shall not be subject to the arbitration provisions set forth in either Article ___ or Section 4 of this Article. The failure or refusal by a Union officer, agent, representative, steward or committeeman to comply with the provisions of Section 1 of this Article constitutes leading and instigating a violation of said Section 1, it being specifically agreed that the Union officers, agents, representatives, stewards and committeemen, by accepting such positions, have assumed the responsibility of affirmatively preventing violations of Section 1 of this Article by reporting to work and performing work as scheduled and/or required by the Company.

Section 3. No-Lockouts. In consideration of the Union's commitment as set forth in Section 1 of this Article, the Company shall not lock out employees.

Section 4. Expedited Arbitration. In the event of an alleged violation of Section 1 of this Article arising out of a matter not subject to resolution pursuant to the grievance and arbitration procedures set forth in Article ___ of this Agreement, the Company may institute expedited arbitration proceedings regarding such alleged violation by delivering written or telegraphic notice thereof to the Union and to the American Arbitration Association. Immediately upon receipt of such written or telegraphic notice, the American Arbitration Association shall appoint an arbitrator to hear the matter. The arbitrator shall determine the time and place of the hearing, give telegraphic notice thereof, and hold the hearing within twenty-four (24) hours after his appointment. The fee and other expenses of the arbitrator in connection with this expedited arbitration proceeding shall be shared equally by the Company and the Union. The failure of either party or any witness to attend the hearing, as scheduled and noticed by the arbitrator, shall not delay the hearing, and the arbitrator shall proceed to take evidence and issue an award and order as though such party or witness were present. The sole issue at the hearing shall be whether a violation of Section 1 of this Article has occurred or is occurring, and the arbitrator shall not consider any matter justifying, explaining or mitigating such violation. If the arbitrator finds that a violation of Section 1 of this Article is occurring or has occurred, he shall issue a cease and desist order with respect to such violation. The arbitrator's written opinion, award and order shall be issued within twenty-four (24) hours after the close of the hearing. Such award and order shall be final and binding on the Company and the Union.

Section 5. Injunctive Relief Pending Expedited Arbitration.

In the event of an alleged violation of Section 1 of this Article to which Section 4 of this Article is applicable, the Company may immediately apply to the United States District Court for the _____ District of _____ for injunctive relief, including a temporary restraining order, prohibiting the continuation of such an alleged violation pending submission of the matter to arbitration and the issuance and enforcement of the arbitrator's order.

Section 6. Damages and Other Remedies. In addition to any other remedy set forth in this Article ___, the Company, without submitting the issue of damages to arbitration, may institute, in any court of competent jurisdiction, an action against the Union for damages suffered by the Company as a result of a violation of this Article ___. The remedies set forth in this Article ___ are not exclusive, and the Company may pursue whatever other remedies are available to it at law or equity.

NO-STRIKE, NO-LOCKOUT (version 2)

Section 1. During the term of this agreement the parties hereto agree that there shall be No-Strikes of any kind whatsoever; work stoppages; slow-downs; or interference or interruption with the production or operations of the plant by any employees or the Union; and there shall be no lock-outs by the Employer.

Section 2. Nor shall there be any strike or interruption of work during the term of this agreement because of any disputes or disagreements between any other persons (or other employers or unions) who are not signatory parties to this agreement.

Section 3. Employees who violate this provision shall be subject to disciplinary action, including discharge; and any claim by either party against the other of a violation of this article shall be subject to arbitration as provided for under Article - of this agreement.

NO-STRIKE, NO-LOCKOUT (version 3)

Section 1. During the term of this Agreement the Company agrees that there shall be No-Lockout. The closing down of the facility or any part thereof or curtailing any operations for business reasons shall not be construed to be a lockout.

Section 2. The Union, its officers, agents, members and employees covered by this Agreement agree that so long as this Agreement is in effect there shall be No-Strikes, sit-downs, slowdowns, stoppages of work, picket lines, boycotts, disturbances of even a momentary nature, or any other acts that interfere with the Company's operations or delivery schedules. Any violation of the foregoing provision may be made the subject of disciplinary action, including discharge, and such acts or the Company's determination of the facts on which such action is based, may not be raised as a grievance under Article ___ of this Agreement.

Section 3. In the event of unauthorized strikes, slowdowns, sit-downs, or other stoppages of work, the Union will take immediate steps, not later than four (4) hours to terminate such conduct. As one of the immediate steps, the Union shall notify employees that the strikes, slowdowns, sit-downs, or other stoppages of work are unauthorized and in violation of the Agreement, and shall order all employees to terminate such conduct. The failure or refusal by the Union to comply with the provision of Section 2 constitutes leading and instigating a violation of Section 2, it being specifically agreed that the Union has assumed the responsibility of affirmatively preventing violations of Section 2 by reporting to work and performing work as scheduled and required by the Company.

NO-STRIKE/NO-LOCKOUT (version 4)
The company agrees that during the life of this agreement there shall be No-Lockouts, and the union agrees that during the life of this agreement there shall be No-Strikes, sit-downs, slowdowns, walkouts or stoppage of work, or impeding the conducting of operations of the company for any reason whatsoever.

NO-STRIKE - NO-LOCKOUT (version 5)
Section 1. During the term of this Agreement or any extension thereof, neither the Union nor any employee covered by the Agreement will instigate, promote, sponsor, engage in, or condone any strike, sympathy strike, slowdown, concerted stoppage of work, or any other intentional interruption of the operations of the Company.
Section 2. The Employer will not lock out any employees covered by this Agreement during the term of the Agreement as a result of a labor dispute with the Union.

NO-STRIKE (version 6)
(A)   During the term of this Agreement, neither the Union nor its officers or agents or any employee, for any reason, will authorize, institute, aid, condone or engage in a slowdown, work stoppage, strike; interfere with the work functions or obligations of the Company.

(B)   The Union agrees to notify all of its local offices and representatives of their obligation and responsibility under this Article and for maintaining compliance with the prohibition against strikes. The Union further agrees to notify employees of these responsibilities, including their responsibility to remain at work during any interruption which may be caused or initiated by others.

(C)   The Company may discharge or discipline any employee who violates the provisions of this Article and the Union will not resort to the Grievance Procedure on such employee's behalf; however, if the issue is whether or not the employee engaged in activities prohibited by this Article, the Union may elect to represent the employee in such grievance through the Grievance Procedure.

(D)   Nothing contained herein shall preclude the Company from obtaining judicial restraint and damages in the event of a violation of this Article.

No Discrimination

No discrimination clauses are common in collective bargaining agreements, but their actual legal effect is somewhat controversial. Most of the time courts allow employees to exercise their rights under federal statutes, although in some cases they will require a case to go through an arbitration procedure first.

Some companies argue that non-discrimination clauses in a contract require employees to process discrimination claims through the grievance procedure instead of the EEOC or state equal employment agency. If the clause in the contract provides the same remedies available under these statutes, some courts agree that the employee only gets one "bite at the apple" and must litigate his or her claim through the labor contract procedure. However, the clause must also contain a "clear and unmistakable" waiver of rights. Even with all these bases covered, some courts still will not allow the union to waive statutory rights of individual employees. For this reason, some employers object to any language at all on the subject, to avoid confusion.

Most contracts include language that prohibits discrimination based on many of the protected classifications under federal and state law. Further, some clauses are much more broad including prohibitions on discrimination based on sexual orientation or other categories not specifically protected under federal law. Finally, most clauses also contain some limitation on discrimination for union membership or engaging in union business. In some cases, this is the only issue discussed in the discrimination clause.

Clause Summaries and Drafting Notes

There are four no discrimination clauses provided as models below. The first is a basic non-discrimination clause. It also contains language regarding gender references in the contract, noting that the pronoun "he" is meant to include men and women. This clause is clearly not broad enough to constitute an effective waiver of statutory claims, and I doubt it would be of much use at all to an employee-member.

The second version is more effective, due primarily to its limited nature. This clause only covers discrimination based on union activity. It states that there will be no discrimination or favoritism to employees because of union activity.

The third version includes sexual orientation and Vietnam veteran status as part of the no-discrimination pledge. Therefore, this clause gives employees greater rights than they would have under federal statute. There is also a statement that there will be no discrimination because of union activity.

The final version states that there will be no discrimination for the reasons provided under state and federal law. It specifically provides that discrimination claims are grievable up to the second step of the grievance process. It states that the union will support the company's ADA and Affirmative Action programs. It also states that there will be no discrimination based on union membership, whether the employee supports or refrains from union activity. This clause is interesting because it provides limited rights under the labor agreement for appeal of discrimination cases, obviously allowing employees to rely on the lower level dispute resolution mechanisms for discrimination cases but then removing them into the federal and state complaint system for these charges, where they would normally be handled in non-union organizations. This is an interesting way to deal with the conflict over whether a grievance procedure gives an employee "two bites of the apple," in effect using the grievance procedure as a mediation process within the company. I like this formulation.

NO DISCRIMINATION (version 1)
Section 1. The Company and the Union agree to abide by applicable laws concerning no discrimination because of race, color, religion, national origin, sex, age and disability. Both parties further agree to abide by all applicable provisions of the National Labor Relations Act, as amended.
Section 2. Any reference to one gender throughout this Agreement applies to both genders, unless otherwise specified.

NO DISCRIMINATION (version 2)
It is understood that the Employer shall show no discrimination against or favoritism among its employees for Union activities or otherwise.

NON-DISCRIMINATION (version 3)
Section 1. In accordance with applicable law, neither the Employer nor the Union shall discriminate against any employee covered by this Agreement because of handicapped, physical or mental condition, race, creed, color, national origin, sex, sexual orientation, age,

parental status, marital status, or political affiliation. Further, the parties agree not to discriminate against disabled veterans and veterans of the Vietnam Era.

Section 2. The Employer will not discriminate against any member, steward, or officer of the Union including those who are participating in negotiations, adjustment of grievances or the performance of committee work which is in the interest of the Union and its members.

NON-DISCRIMINATION (Version 4)
Section 1. Non-Discrimination (State & Federal Law).

(A)   The Company and the Union shall not discriminate against any employee for any reason prohibited under State or Federal Law.

(B)   The Union shall have the right to consult on issues of discrimination or unlawful discrimination with the Step 1 Management Representative and/or his designee(s), up through the Step 2 Management Representative and/or his designee(s), to the Human Resources Department.

(C)   Any claim of discrimination or unlawful discrimination by an employee against the Company, its officials or representatives, except for grievances related to Union membership, shall only be subject to the method of review prescribed by law or by rules and regulations having the force and effect of law.

(D)   The Union agrees to support the Company's current affirmative action programs and efforts to comply with the Americans with Disabilities Act.

Section 2. - Non-Discrimination (Union Membership).

Neither the Company nor the Union shall interfere with the right of employees covered by this Agreement to become or refrain from becoming members of the Union, and neither the Company nor the Union shall discriminate against any such employee because of membership or non-membership in any employee organization.

Union Business

Another important compromise deals with the employer's property rights versus the union's right to meet, confer and communicate with members. The union is obviously interested in protecting its right to access to its members in order to investigate grievances, discuss potential contract violations, learn about needs and interests of members and otherwise administer the collective bargaining agreement and the business affairs of the union. The company, on the other hand, has a significant interest in maintaining its operations without interruption or disruption by union officials. For this reason, the company tends to want to restrict access to its property and its employees as much as possible.

Clause Summaries and Drafting Notes

Based on these issues the company and union will attempt to reach an agreement on how to best accommodate each side's interest. The key issues that are discussed in these clauses are:

- Who has authority on the part of the union to enter the employer's property and discuss issues with members?
- When, if ever, these meetings may take place on the employer's property
- Whether or not the union will have the right to communicate to employees in writing via either distribution or, more commonly, a bulletin board

There a number of creative ways in which these various issues and interests are resolved in labor agreements.

There are four model clauses on union access. The first version is a very strong company provision. It essentially requires all union business to be conducted during non-working hours and in non-work areas. In cases where meetings are requested the company property (in a company meeting room, for example), the meeting must be cleared with management.

The second version strictly limits who has authority to meet with members and investigate grievances on behalf of the union. The union is required to notify the company before those individuals can meet with members. The clause also strictly describes the type, location and material that may be posted on the union-provided bulletin board on the company's property. The clause gives the union the right to meet with members in public areas as well as in private areas if arranged with management. The clause also provides for record access as well as for quarterly meetings between the four union representatives and the plant manager. The company is required to respond in writing to the issues that are brought up during these quarterly meetings. This clause is very extensive. If tilted at all, it is probably more of a pro-union clause.

The third version is brief and more problematic for the company. It provides for a bulletin board as well as the company's right to remove material that is "inflammatory or controversial." While on its face this language seems relatively strong for the company, it does provide a lot of room for interpretation as to what constitutes "inflammatory" material. In the end the company may have little right to remove material from the bulletin board. The provision also provides union access with prior notice, also a good provision for the company. However, it states that such access will not be denied unreasonably (the access cannot interfere with company operations). Again, there is a lot of room for interpretation and potential conflict on this issue. Overall this clause seems most likely to lead to grievances and arbitrations if the company denies access or removes something from the bulletin board.

Finally, the fourth version deals primarily with the rights of bargaining committee members. It states that the bargaining committee will have an opportunity to meet, with pay, prior to contract negotiation sessions for preparation as well as the right to meet with pay during contract negotiations. It caps the total amount of paid time for contract preparation and negotiations to 500 hours. It further provides that the employer may limit the number of employees from any particular work area that can work on negotiations. Finally, it gives employees the right to request leave without pay for union conventions and other meetings and provides that the employer will only deny these requests in writing based on business necessity. These provisions are very favorable to the union.

UNION BUSINESS (version 1)
The Union agrees that it will not conduct Union business during working hours and that requests for meeting room space must be cleared through the Employee Relations Officer.

UNION BUSINESS (version 2)
Section 1. Definitions. The term "Grievance Representative," as used in this Agreement, shall mean

a bargaining unit employee covered by this Agreement who has been designated by the President of the Union to investigate grievances at the Oral Step and to represent grievant at the Oral Step and Step 1 meetings on grievances which have been properly filed under Article 6 of this Agreement, when the Union has been selected as the employee's representative.

Section 2. Designation of Employee Representatives.

(A)   The President of the Union shall furnish to the Company and keep up-to-date a list of Union Staff Representatives. The Company will not recognize any person as a Staff Representative whose name does not appear on the list.

(B)   From employees in the bargaining unit, the Union shall select a reasonable number of Union Grievance Representatives. The Union shall furnish the Company the name, social security number, official class title, name of employing agency, and specific work location of each employee who has been designated to act as a Grievance Representative. The Company shall not recognize an employee as an authorized Grievance Representative until such information has been received from the Union.

Section 3. Bulletin Boards.

(A)   Where requested in writing, the Company agrees to furnish in Company-controlled facilities to which bargaining unit employees are assigned, wall space not to exceed "24x36" for Union-purchased bulletin boards of an equal size. Such bulletin boards will be placed at a Company facility in an area normally accessible to, and frequented by, covered employees. Once a location has been established, it shall not be moved without notice. Where the Union currently maintains bulletin boards or bulletin board space that practice shall continue.

(B) The use of Union bulletin board space is limited to the following notices:
   a. Recreational and social affairs of the Union
   b. Union meetings
   c. Union elections
   d. Reports of Union committees
   e. Union benefit programs
   f. Current Union Agreement
   g. Training and educational opportunities
   h. Decisions reached through consultation meetings, as approved by the Department of Human Resources
   i. Notices of wage increases for covered employees

(C) Materials posted on these bulletin boards shall not contain anything which violates or has the effect of violating any law, rule, or regulation, nor shall any posted material contain anything reflecting adversely on the Company, or any of its officers or employees.

(D) Postings must be dated and bear the signature of an authorized Union representative.

(E) A violation of these provisions by a Union Staff Representative or an authorized representative shall be a basis for removal of bulletin board privileges for that representative by the Department of Human Resources.

Section 4. Information.

(A) Upon request of the President of the Union, or

their designee, the Company will, no more than on a quarterly basis, provide the Union with a list giving the name, home address on file, classification title, and gross salary for each employee in this bargaining Unit. This list will be prepared on the basis of the latest information on file at the time the list is prepared.

(B)   The Union agrees that all home addresses and telephone numbers of bargaining unit employees shall remain confidential. The Union will not disclose the home addresses and telephone numbers of bargaining unit members to third parties including, but not limited to, sale of the information to other persons or parties.

Section 5. Representative Access.

(A)   The Company agrees that accredited representatives of the Union, shall have access to the premises of the Company, which are available to the public.

(B)   If any area of the Company's premises is restricted to the public, permission must be requested to enter such areas and such permission will not be unreasonably denied. Such access shall be during the regular working hours of the employee and shall be to investigate an employee's grievance.

(C)   Upon request and receipt of payment, the Company shall provide accredited representatives information, documents, or other public records for the investigation of an employee's grievance.

Section 6. Consultation.

(A)   In order to provide a means for continuing

communication between the parties and upon request of the President of the Union, the Director of Human Resources and not more than three (3) representatives of the Union shall meet and consult quarterly. Such meetings shall be held at a time and place designated by the Department of Human Resources.

(B) Upon request by the designated Union Staff Representative, the Plant Manager and the Staff Representative, with not more than three (3) Union representatives, shall make a good faith effort to meet and consult quarterly. Such meetings shall be held at a time and place to be designated by the Plant Manager or his designee after consulting with the Union Staff Representative.

(C) Upon request by the designated Union Staff Representative, the Step 1 Management Representative and/or his designee(s) and the designated Union Staff Representative, with not more than two (2) Union representatives from the Agency, shall make a good faith effort to meet and consult. Such meetings shall be held at a time and place to be designated by the Step 1 Management Representative after consulting with the Union Staff Representative. A copy of all requests shall be served on both the Agency and the Union at their principal offices.

(D) All consultation meetings will be scheduled after giving due consideration to the availability and work location of all parties. If a consultation meeting is held or requires reasonable travel time during the working hours of any employee participant, such participant shall be excused without loss of pay for that purpose. Attendance at a consultation meeting outside of regular working hours shall not be deemed time worked.

(E)   The purpose of all consultation meetings shall be to discuss matters relating to the administration of this Agreement and any Company activities affecting unit employees. It is understood that these meetings shall not be used for the purpose of discussing pending grievances or for negotiation purposes. The parties shall exchange agenda indicating the matters they wish to discuss no later than five (5) calendar days prior to the scheduled meeting date.

(F)   An agency shall prepare a written response to issues raised during a consultation meeting within thirty (30) days after the date of the meeting.

Section 7. Negotiations. The Union agrees that all collective bargaining is to be conducted with Company representatives designated for that purpose. The Company and the Union may mutually agree to meet at a Company facility or other location, which involves no rental cost to the Company. There shall be no negotiation by the Union at any other level of Company.

UNION BUSINESS (version 3)

Section 1. Bulletin Boards. Company agrees to provide bulletin board access for official union business for such materials as announcements of Union meetings, social functions, nomination and election of Union officers, etc. Inflammatory or controversial material may be removed by the Company.

Section 2. Union Access. An officer or business

representative of Teamster Local ____ shall be admitted to the property provided such representative shall comply with the rules and regulations of the Company and shall not interfere with the conduct of the Company's operations. Notice and approval for such visit will be obtained from a Company officer or General Manager. Approval will not be withheld unreasonably.

UNION BUSINESS (version 4)
Section 1. Negotiation Committee.

(A)   The Union may designate certain employees within this unit to serve as its Negotiation Committee, and such employees will be granted administrative leave to attend negotiating sessions with the Company. An employee serving on the Negotiation Committee shall also be granted a maximum of eight (8) hours administrative leave to attend a negotiation preparatory meeting to be held the calendar day immediately preceding each scheduled negotiation session, provided that the negotiation preparatory meeting is held on what would otherwise be the employee's normal workday. No individual employee shall be credited with more than the number of hours in the employee's regular workday for any day the employee is in negotiations. The total number of hours, including the hours spent in negotiation preparatory meetings, paid all employees on the Union's Negotiation Committee shall not exceed five hundred (500) hours. The time in attendance at such preparatory meetings and negotiating sessions shall not be counted as hours worked for the purpose of computing compensatory time or overtime. The Company shall not reimburse the employee for travel, meals, lodging, or any expense incurred in connection with attendance at preparatory meetings or negotiating sessions.

(B) No more than two (2) employees shall be selected from the same work unit at any one time, nor shall the selection of any employee unduly hamper the operations of the work unit.

Section 2. Union Activities. Employees covered by this Agreement shall have the right to request leave without pay for the purpose of attending Union conventions, conferences and meetings. When such requests cannot be granted, the supervisor shall provide such denial in writing.

Tool Allowance

Many contracts, particularly in manufacturing or building trades, provide for tool allowances. These clauses outline the company's responsibility (if any) for providing tools and/or compensating employees for tools. The key interests at stake in these clauses are:

- ❑ The company's and employee's interest in ensuring access to the tools they necessary to do the job effectively and safely
- ❑ The company's interest in making sure that tools are cared for properly and that employees are good stewards
- ❑ The union's interest in making sure employees are not required to provide tools that they feel should be provided by the company

Clause Summaries and Drafting Notes

These clauses are very specific to their operations. I include two here as examples. The first version states that the company will provide all "necessary" tools. Whether a tool is necessary or not is decided by the company foreman. This is a typical provision that leaves only open for interpretation the finality of the foreman's decision. The company can strengthen the clause even further by noting that the foreman's decision is final and binding and not subject to the grievance procedure.

The second version of the tool allowance clause states that no employee is required to provide his own tools and that the company will provide all tools "necessary to perform the job." Again, the question is what tools are necessary and under what circumstances the employee may argue with the foreman's assessment.

TOOL ALLOWANCE (version 1)

The Company shall furnish and replace necessary tools. Necessary tools to be determined by the Foreman.

TOOL ALLOWANCE (version 2)

No employee is required to furnish any tools. The Employer will furnish such tools that are necessary for the performance of the employee's job.

Uniforms

Unions and companies sometimes include language about uniforms where those are provided or are required to perform the job. The main issues discussed in these clauses relate to whether uniforms are required, who provides the uniforms, and what happens when a uniform wears out or is lost. Occasionally these clauses will also describe the employee's obligations to wear a particular uniform.

Clause Summaries and Drafting Notes

There are three model uniform clauses. The first version states that the company will provide 11 uniforms and a winter jacket. There is also a provision regarding ID cards that the company will replace if worn out; if lost the employee is responsible to replacement. This clause does not explain what happens if a uniform is lost, stolen or wears out. I would add a provision like the one for lost ID cards if drafting a counter-proposal to this clause.

The second version states that the uniform is provided and that employees receive a $250 uniform maintenance allowance or a cleaning service provided by the company (but not both). There is also a shoe allowance of $75. This clause differs from the first in that it sets budgetary amounts, but it does not necessarily provide for specific numbers of uniforms or types of shoes to be worn.

Version three states that the company will provide three sets of uniforms and even goes into detail, requiring at least one set of pants and shirt. Employees in this organization also receive a jacket. This clause does state that the company will replace a uniform that is worn out and turned in by the employee. Again, it does not specifically state what happens if the employee loses a uniform or claims it is stolen. Presumably given the language regarding the replacement, this would be responsibility of the employee, but it is not laid out specifically in the clause. This would be an area for the company to tighten up the language in a proposal.

UNIFORMS (version 1)
Section 1. The Company will supply eleven (11) uniforms year-round.
Section 2. One (1) winter jacket, size extra-large, will be provided in the shop for use by the Automotive Mechanics.
Section 3. I.D. cards will be replaced at no cost if it becomes worn out (old I.D. must be turned in). Cost of replacing lost I.D. cards will be the responsibility of the employee.

UNIFORMS (version 2)
Section 1. Uniforms. Employees shall receive a standard issue uniform and uniform accessories.
Section 2. Uniform Maintenance Allowance. The Company will provide employees who are furnished and required to wear a uniform, a maintenance allowance in the amount of $250.00 annually, unless laundry and dry cleaning facilities are available and the service is furnished by the Company without cost to the employee; in addition, employees shall receive a shoe allowance in the amount of $75.00 annually.

UNIFORMS (version 3)

The Employer will provide three (3) sets of work clothing per employee consisting of pants and shirts or coveralls. However, at least one uniform will consist of one set of pants and shirt. In addition, each employee will receive one all-purpose jacket. Cleaning and maintenance of this clothing is the responsibility of the individual employee. The Employer will replace all such worn out uniforms upon turn-in of such clothing by employee.

Savings Clause

The savings clause is designed for the rare occasion where one clause or part of a collective bargaining agreement is found to be unlawful by a court or government agency. In these rare instances there is a question about whether the contract remains in effect and whether the parties have to negotiate over the now changed collective bargaining agreement. Many times, companies and unions will include a savings clause that formally sets out how such a situation will be handled by the parties.

Clause Summaries and Drafting Notes

Most saving clauses will discuss the following key aspects:

- ❏ What types of rulings will result in the use of the savings clause (federal, state or local statutes, court decisions and the like)?
- ❏ What is considered a "final ruling" and the impact of an appeal
- ❏ The effect of these decisions (i.e. whether the contract remains in effect or is re-opened for negotiation)

There are four model savings clauses described below. The first version is a general savings clause that states that if a clause violates state or federal law the rest of the agreement stays in effect. This clause is somewhat vague and also narrow. It does not deal with court decisions and does not specifically discuss whether there would be negotiations or re-opener of the contract in the case of a state or federal change that prohibits part of the contract.

Version two states that if a contract clause violates a "subsequently enacted" legislation or "court decision" that the remainder of the agreement will stay in effect. It also contains re-opener language limited to the clause invalidated by the enactment or court decision. This clause also has some problems. First, there is the question of what happens if legislation is not "subsequently enacted" but was in place at the time that the contract was entered. Also, it is a good idea to clarify what kind of court decision will be considered a final – since many court decisions can be appealed. If a lower court rules that a clause is invalid, and that decision is appealed does the savings clause re-opener provision take effect?

Version three is more specific but not necessarily clearer. It states that federal, state laws or agency decisions are covered by the clause. It contains final agreement language (see the zipper clause summaries below) and states that where part of the agreement is invalidated the remainder of the contract stays in effect. However, this clause does not discuss court decisions. It also does not say what happens to the specific clause that is invalidated i.e. there is no re-opener language. These vague areas could lead to significant problems or arbitrations.

The fourth version states that an invalid clause has no effect on the remainder of the agreement but has no re-opener language. It mentions specifically the change of laws, court decisions and existing or subsequent legislation, so it covers a broad range of possible changes. This is superior to the other clauses listed above. The lack of re-opener language can be an advantage or disadvantage depending on the situation. Since the parties can agree to bargain at any time, the real issue is whether the company or union wants the ability to <u>compel</u> the other side to negotiate. This is a very fact-dependent decision.

SAVINGS CLAUSE (version 1)
In the event any Federal or State Law conflicts with any provision of this Agreement, the provision or provisions so affected shall no longer be operative or binding upon the parties, but the remaining portion of the Agreement shall remain in full force and effect.

SAVINGS CLAUSE (version 2)
Should any part hereof or any provision herein contained be rendered or declared invalid by reason of any existing or subsequently enacted legislation or by any decree of a court of competent jurisdiction, such invalidation of such part or portion of this Agreement shall not invalidate the remaining portion hereof; provided, however, upon such invalidation the parties agree to meet and negotiate such parts or provisions affected. The remaining part or provisions shall remain in full force and effect.

SAVINGS (version 3)
Section 1. This Agreement shall not supersede:
(A)   Applicable Federal and State laws as such laws may become amended from time to time;
(B)   Rules of Federal and State agencies which have the force and effect of law, as such may be amended from time to time
Section 2. This Agreement constitutes the entire Agreement and understanding between the parties and

supersedes all prior written and oral agreements (commitments and practices) between the Employer, Union and the employees. This Agreement expresses all obligations of, and restrictions imposed on each of the parties during the term of the Agreement.

Section 3. Should any provision of this Agreement or any application thereof become unlawful by virtue of any Federal or State law, Executive Order or decision of a court of competent jurisdiction, the provision or application shall be modified by the parties to comply with the law, order or decision and all other provisions of this Agreement shall continue in full force and effect.

SAVINGS (version 4)

If any provision of this Agreement is in contravention of the laws or regulations of the United States or the State of [State], by reason of any court action or existing or subsequently enacted legislation which is in conflict with a provision of this Agreement then such provision shall not be applicable, performed or enforced; but the remaining parts or portions of this Agreement shall remain in full force and effect for the term of this Agreement.

Assignability

Assignability provisions are relatively common in business contracts. They are somewhat less important in labor contracts because the general concept of assignability is typically covered in more detail in a "successorship" clause (see more on these below). The basic concept is that the rights and responsibilities of the parties cannot be assigned to the other parties without the express written consent of both parties. There is one relatively straightforward sample clause below.

ASSIGNABILITY

This Agreement is not assignable by either of the parties hereto without the written authorization of the other party first had and obtained.

Work by Non-Bargaining Unit Employees

Bargaining unit work performed by managers and other non-unit employees, along with the subcontracting clauses that follow, are often a critical issue to unions. The key concerns with these two types of clauses is protecting the union's monopoly over the provision of labor within a company. The performance of bargaining unit work by supervisors, managers, temporary employees, casual employees or others tends to dilute the power of the labor organization within the company. Over a long period of time the practice may also dilute the financial power of the union by replacing dues paying union members with non-dues paying individuals.

The union's interest in protecting its monopoly on the labor force is countered by the company's interest in having flexibility to get its work done in any way possible. Certainly in emergencies the company often wants to ensure that it has the ability to fill the needs of its customers whether with bargaining unit employees or supervisors or managers. These clauses will often contain some exceptions for emergency situations.

Clause Summaries and Drafting Notes

The main issues discussed in these clauses are under what circumstances, if any, the company can use non-bargaining unit employees to perform work normally performed within the bargaining unit. Common details include:
- Whether the company must notify the union in advance of using non-bargaining unit employees
- What constitutes an "emergency" in clauses that give the right to substitute non-bargaining unit

labor in emergency situations
- ❑ What specifically constitutes "bargaining unit work" under the agreement
- ❑ Call-back procedures or penalties to be paid by management if bargaining unit employees are not called in when available

There are two versions of these clauses provided. Version one is a very strong management version of a non-bargaining unit employee clause. It states that supervisors and managers can work doing bargaining unit tasks even if those sometimes are physically identical to the work being performed under the collective bargaining agreement. It states that supervisors and other non-covered individuals can work without limitation in these areas. This is strong management language.

Version two states that non-bargaining unit employees cannot work except for in cases of emergency. The clause specifically defines emergency as such situations that are beyond the control of the employer and for which there could not be any pre-planning. This clause is much more favorable to the union and one can imagine that the definition of emergency could be constructed very restrictively, prohibiting management from using non-bargaining unit personnel except in the most extreme and unplanned situations.

<u>WORK PERFORMED BY NON-BARGAINING UNIT PERSONNEL (version 1)</u>
The parties understand that the nature of the business requires that non-bargaining unit personnel may be required to perform a variety of duties which are

---

similar in nature, and in some cases physically identical, to those performed by bargaining unit personnel. The parties therefore agree that supervisory personnel and other personnel not within the bargaining unit covered by this Agreement shall be permitted to perform without limitation that work ordinarily performed by employees within the bargaining unit described in Article ___ of this Agreement.

WORK PERFORMED BY NON-BARGAINING UNIT PERSONNEL (version 2)
No supervisor nor salaried employee shall perform any of the work covered under this Agreement except in cases of emergency. Emergency is defined as a situation beyond the control of the Employer for which it could not preplan.

Subcontracting

Subcontracting clauses again deal with the union's interest in the monopoly on labor versus the company's interest in flexibility. Instead of limiting the use of personnel from within the organization, these clauses deal with the use of subcontractors to perform work normally performed by members of the bargaining unit. Unions normally wish to restrict this practice as much as possible hoping to prevent any subcontracting of work. Where unions will sometimes compromise on the issue, they typically want to include language that says that any subcontracting will not affect current bargaining unit positions.

Clause Summaries and Drafting Notes

There are two model versions of subcontracting clauses. The first version states that subcontracting is only allowed if the facility is filled to capacity. This is a common way for unions to limit the use of subcontractors except in emergency or over capacity situations. It states that any work that is given to another facility must be given to a facility with a union contract. It also states that employees will not be required to perform struck work. This clause is very restrictive and is favorable to the union.

Version two gives the company the right to subcontract where it deems that the use of its own equipment is not appropriate for the business demands. It also provides that management can perform bargaining unit duties in situations where all other operators are working or unavailable to work. It gives, under certain circumstances, the ability to contract aspects of the company's operation (in this case a bus company can subcontract towing and maintenance of its equipment at the discretion of the foreman). This clause is still somewhat restrictive of subcontracting, but much more expansive than the clause in version one. This is a more typical compromise in labor agreements.

SUBCONTRACTING (version 1)
No work done in the plant shall be given out unless the mill giving out such work is filled to capacity on its normal shift operations. In any case where work may be given out, such work must be given to a mill having a contract with the Union. Workers shall not be required to perform my work for any mill or firm in which there is a strike.

SUBCONTRACTING (version 2)
Section 1. Bus trips may be contracted out when use of Company vehicles is not appropriate as determined by the Transportation Manager.

Section 2. The Transportation Manager, or other qualified Company personnel, when all Motor Vehicle Operator/Mechanics are already working or are unavailable for duty, shall be able to perform driving duties.

Section 3. Towing of vehicles, maintenance, and/or repairs may be subcontracted when the Company does not have the equipment necessary to properly perform such service. The Garage Foreman will determine if the Company possesses such equipment and if/when the service can be provided.

Section 4. Maintenance or repairs may be subcontracted when Transportation Department personnel do not possess the knowledge and expertise necessary to properly perform said maintenance or repair. The Garage Foreman will determine if Transportation Department personnel possess said knowledge and expertise.

Past Practice
Past practice is one of the most important concepts in the administration of labor agreements and can make or break most arbitration cases. Past practice clauses, however, are not very common as separate clauses in labor agreements. The idea of the clause is to state clearly how prior working conditions will be treated as past practice.

This clause is intended to instruct future arbitrators more than either of the two parties. It acts as a point of reference for an arbitrator when determining the company's past practice. Sometimes similar language is included within an arbitration clause as part of the limitations on the arbitrator. The clause is also designed to "set in stone" working conditions that are not covered in the collective bargaining agreement specifically. This type of clause is much more favorable to a union than to a company. Companies will typically want to keep their flexibility to change things that were in place prior to the collective bargaining agreement being entered so long as there is not a specific clause prohibiting that in the collective bargaining agreement.

Clause Summaries and Drafting Notes
The past practice clause below fixes not only wages but also "fixed financial arrangements" and prohibits them from being changed or reduced during the term of the collective bargaining agreement. The same restriction applies to local rules in effect at the time of the agreement. This, in effect, is a "reverse zipper" clause, prohibiting management from making changes to anything during the term of the contract. Further it opens the door for negotiation during the term of the

agreement on any working conditions that are frozen by the past practice clause. The clause overall is very restrictive to management and is not recommended.

PAST PRACTICE
It is specifically agreed that all weekly wages, salaries, and other fixed financial arrangements of employees in effect at the date hereof or increased hereafter by mutual agreement shall not be reduced.

Local rules or regulations covering working practices and working conditions of employees which have been established by custom or local agreement and were in effect prior to the execution of this agreement, shall not be changed during the life of this agreement without mutual consent. It is understood, however, that the company or the union, through their representatives, or committees, or in such manner as they may elect, may at any time discuss and negotiate for changes in said local rules or regulations covering working practices and working conditions of employees in the plant which have been established by custom or local agreement, were in effect prior to the execution of this agreement, and are not in conflict with this agreement.

Zipper Clause

A zipper clause is the opposite of the past practice clause we reviewed above. It is a way to ensure that anything that is not specifically included in the collective bargaining agreement is not open for negotiation during the term of the agreement. It is also a way, in conjunction with management rights clause, to help ensure that the company has the right to act independently in areas that are not specifically restricted by the collective bargaining agreement. At issue is the company's interest in making clear the limited nature of the compromise of its management rights. The union, on the other hand, hopes to prevent the company from changing work conditions during the term of the contract.

Clause Summaries and Drafting Notes

The company's basic goal with a zipper clause is to limit restrictions on its right to manage to those specifically described in the collective bargaining agreement. The remainder of the company's management rights remain, and the company can make changes at will in these "non-restricted" areas. Unions, on the other hand, hope to prevent management from making unilateral changes in working conditions during the term of the agreement. They will either object to any zipper language in its entirety or attempt to water down the zipper clause proposed by the company.

There are three model clauses below. The first version states specifically that both parties had the unlimited right to make demands and proposals and waive their rights without qualification to bargain over issues during the term of the agreement, even if conditions change in such a way that the parties did not contemplate during negotiations. The clause states that the company has the right to make changes specifically in any of those areas that are not in the agreement. This is a strong pro-management zipper clause.

The second version also contains entire agreement language stating that all demands are settled as stated in the contract and includes a union waiver to discuss issues whether they are in the contract or not. This clause, while also strong, is somewhat more vague than the first version. Although it waives the right to "discuss" does not necessarily give the company the right to make changes in these areas. It is just not as tight as the first version.

Version three has language stating that the contract supersedes all other agreements and constitutes the entire agreement of the parties. It has waiver language stating that the company and the union have the unlimited right to bargain and make proposals, thereby limiting their right to argue about changes during the term of the contract. However, this clause has specific re-opener language for four clauses in the second year and an additional four clauses in the third year of the agreement. This language is uncommon but depending how it is used could be helpful. The downside of such language is that it specifically grants the union the ability to re-open contract negotiations each year. On the other hand, outside of those four clauses, changes cannot be bargained by the union because the union was given specific authority to bargain only in those four areas of its choosing. The agreement itself says that there is an unqualified waiver outside of these specific re-openers. The clause further gives the union the right to settle grievances using letters of understanding without going to the bargaining committee. Overall this is an interesting clause and relatively strong for management with the exception of the re-opener language which certainly could present problems depending on the circumstances; it seems like a pretty solid compromise where a union flatly refuses to a complete zipper.

ENTIRE AGREEMENT (Zipper) (version 1)

Section 1. The parties acknowledge that during the negotiations which resulted in this Agreement, each had the unlimited right and opportunity to make demands and proposals with respect to all proper subjects of collective bargaining and that all such subjects have been discussed and negotiated upon and the Agreements contained in this Agreement were arrived at after the free exercise of such rights and opportunities. Therefore, the Company and the Union, for the life of this Agreement, each voluntarily and unqualifiedly waive the right and each agrees the other shall not be obligated to bargain collectively with respect to any subject or matter not specifically referred to or covered in this Agreement, even though such subject or matter may not have been within the knowledge or contemplation of either or both of the parties at the time they negotiated or signed this Agreement.

Section 2. The parties understand and agree that this Agreement covers all bargained for conditions of employment, and that the Company has the right, at its discretion, to change, modify or amend conditions of employment not so covered as its business judgment dictates.

ENTIRE AGREEMENT (Zipper) (version 2)
The parties agree that this agreement constitutes the entire contract between them governing the rates of pay and working conditions of the employees in the bargaining unit during the term hereof and settles all demands and issues on all matters subject to collective bargaining, including any demands made by the Union during negotiations.

Accordingly, the Union expressly waives the right during the term of this agreement to demand, discuss, or negotiate upon any subject matter, whether or not such subject matter is specifically contained in this agreement or whether such subject matter has or has not been raised or discussed by either party during the negotiations leading up to the execution of this agreement.

ENTIRE AGREEMENT (Partial Zipper) (version 3)
Section 1. Agreement/Re-openers.
(A)   This Agreement, upon ratification, supersedes and cancels all prior practices and agreements, whether written or oral, unless expressly stated to the contrary herein, and constitutes the complete and entire agreement between the parties, and concludes collective bargaining for its term.

(B)   The parties acknowledge that, during the negotiations which resulted in this Agreement, each had the unlimited right and opportunity to make demands and proposals with respect to any subject or matter not removed by law from the area of collective bargaining, and that the understandings and agreements arrived at by the parties after the exercise of that right and opportunity are set forth in this Agreement.

(C)   The Company and the Union agree that changes in any four (4) articles within this Agreement that the Union or the Company desire to re-open shall be subject to negotiations for Fiscal Year 2003-2004, plus any articles under study.

(D)   The Company and the Union further agree that changes in any four (4) articles within this Agreement that the Union or the Company desire to re-open shall be subject to negotiations during the second year of this Agreement for Fiscal Year 2004-2005.

(E)   Except as to the above subjects, the Company and the Union, for the duration of this Agreement, each voluntarily and unqualifiedly waives the right, and each agrees that the other shall not be obligated to bargain collectively with respect to any subject or matter referred to, or covered in this Agreement, even though such subjects or matters may not have been within the knowledge or contemplation of either or both of the parties at the time they negotiated or signed this Agreement.

Section 2. Memorandum of Understanding/Settlements. The parties recognize that during the term of this Agreement situations may arise which require terms and conditions not specifically and clearly set forth in the Agreement must be clarified or amended. Under such circumstances, the

Union is specifically authorized by bargaining unit employees to enter into the settlement of grievance disputes or memorandums of understanding which clarify or amend this Agreement, without having to be ratified by bargaining unit members.

Waiver

A waiver clause simply states the impact that a waiver of rights under one section or at one time will have in the future. There is one example of a waiver clause provided here and it simply states the waiver by either party of a provision is not to be considered a waiver for future situations, but it is limited to the one time that the waiver occurred. It states that the agreement is not modified but the actions or omissions of a party and that the fact that a party waives its right in a particular circumstance does not change the agreement.

Whether an arbitrator would give effect to such a clause is questionable. Given facts where one party has clearly and expressly waived its right to complain of a contract violation, it is doubtful most arbitrators would enforce the clause later just because of this language.

WAIVER

The waiver by either party of any provisions or requirements of this agreement shall not be deemed a waiver of such provisions or requirements for the future and shall not constitute a modification of this agreement.

Duration
Duration language is important in a number of ways. Most fundamentally it states how long the contact remains in effect. In addition, it also gives the employer and the union the specific right to re-open the contract for negotiations in the future. Typically these clauses also contain what is known as "evergreen" language that continues a contract on a year-to-year basis if the parties do not agree to re-open the contract for negotiations.

"Evergreen" language is very important in a situation where, for example, the employees in a bargaining unit are interested in decertifying. If employees fail to file a petition within the proper window period and the contract is not reopened for negotiations then the contract bar rule prevents a decertification petition from being entered during the successive one-year terms. The only way to break the cycle is for the company or to notify the other party that it wants the agreement to terminate and to re-open for future negotiations.

Clause Summaries and Drafting Notes
Among the key issues often included in these clauses are:
- ❏ How long will the agreement remain in effect? Most contracts are for 3 years (a union's majority status cannot be questioned during the first 3 years of a contract) but many contracts today are 5 or more years in duration
- ❏ What happens if the contract is not re-opened? This is normally dealt with using an "evergreen" year-to-year extension provision

- Are there any rules the parties must follow to notify of an intention to let the current contract expire to negotiate a new one?
- What happens to the contract rights if the agreement is allowed to terminate? Does it expire completely, or do the terms and conditions remain in effect during the negotiations?

There are three versions of duration clauses included. The first version contains a 60-day notice provision for renewal, otherwise a one-year renewal evergreen clause included. It states that after termination of the agreement all rights under the contract terminate and do not survive. This is important language to extinguish rights that could be subject to future arbitrations. It also prevents an arbitrator from taking up matters that occur after the conclusion or termination of the collective bargaining agreement.

Version two specifically states the time and dates of expiration. It states that it supersedes prior agreements and also contains entire agreement language (like the zipper clauses discussed earlier). It states that a party can initiate negotiations for the next succeeding agreement no earlier than 90 days prior to expiration but does not contain specific language on when the parties must notify that they intend to renegotiate a new agreement. Presumably under this language the company can notify the union days before the contract expires that they intend to negotiate a new agreement. This clause also does not contain evergreen language; this means that if the new contract is not entered into then the current agreement expires.

This language is relatively strong for management.

Version three also states the dates of expiration and contains a year-to-year evergreen clause if the parties fail to reopen the contract for negotiation. They give a specific notification date (September 1 of each year) and state that the parties may also have the right to extend the agreement in writing. Finally, the clause states that the company and the union can terminate or modify the agreement so long as they give the other party not less than 10 days notification of the desired termination date.

DURATION (version 1)

Section 1. This Agreement shall be effective as of _____, 20___, and shall remain in full force and effect until its expiration date, _____.

Section 2. On or before sixty (60) days prior to the expiration date set forth above, either party hereto may notify the other party in writing of its desire to negotiate the terms and provisions of a successor Agreement. If neither of the parties hereto gives notice to the other party of its desire to negotiate a successor Agreement prior to the expiration date of this Agreement as herein provided, this Agreement shall automatically be renewed for successive one (1) year terms thereafter.

Section 3. Upon termination of this agreement, all rights and benefits hereunder shall be terminated and shall not survive the agreement.

DURATION (version 2)

Section 1. This Agreement is effective 12:01 a.m. [Start Date] and expires on 11:59 p.m. [End Date].

Section 2. This Agreement constitutes the sole and entire existing Agreement between the parties hereto and supersedes all prior agreements, commitments, or practices between the Employer, the Union, and the employees, and expresses all obligations of and restrictions imposed on each of the respective parties during its term. **Section 3.** Except as specifically and expressly provided in this Agreement, neither party is required to negotiate any issue during the term of this Agreement. No earlier than 90 days prior to the expiration of this Agreement, either party may initiate negotiation of a successor agreement.

DURATION (version 3)
Section 1. Term.
(A)   This Agreement shall be effective as of the first day of July 20__ and shall remain in full force and effect through the thirtieth day of June 20__. This Agreement shall be automatically renewed from year-to-year thereafter, unless either party shall notify the other in writing on or before September 1 of each year that it desires to change or modify this Agreement. This Agreement shall remain in full force and be effective during the period of negotiation and may be extended in the manner set forth in the following paragraph.

(B)   In the event that the Company and the Union fail to secure a successor Agreement prior to the expiration date of this Agreement, the parties may mutually agree in writing to extend this Agreement for any period of time.

Section 2. Notices.

(A)   In the event that either party desires to terminate or modify this Agreement, written notice must be given to the other party not less than ten (10) days prior to the desired termination date, which shall not be before the anniversary date set forth in Section 1 above.

(B)   Notices thereunder shall be given by registered or certified mail, and if by the Company shall be addressed to [Address]; and if by the Union shall be addressed to [Address]. Either party may, by a like written notice, change the address to which such notice shall be given. Notices shall be considered to have been given as of the date shown on the postmark.

Index

Drafting Notes

About Phillip B. Wilson

Phillip B. Wilson, President of Labor Relations Institute and the founder of Approachable Leadership. He is a national expert on leadership, labor relations, and creating positive workplaces. He is regularly featured in the business media including Fox Business, Bloomberg News, HR Magazine, and the New York Tines.

Phil is the author of more than a dozen books and publications, including his most recent The Approachability Playbook: 3 Essential Habits for Thriving Leaders and Teams and Left of Boom: Putting Proactive Engagement to Work (which reached #2 on Amazon's Hot HR Books list). Wilson is also a highly regarded keynote speaker, delivering keynotes, workshops and webinars regularly for audiences and companies across North America. His publications and speeches cover a wide range of labor, employee relations and leadership topics for both represented and union-free organizations.

Phil practiced labor and employment law in Chicago after earning his J.D. from University of Michigan Law School and remains licensed in the State of Illinois. He remains active in the American Bar Association's Labor and Employment Law Section.

Phil is a recognized thought leader on labor, positive employee relations, and leadership topics. He serves on the Society of Human Resources special Labor Expertise Panel, the US Chamber of Commerce Labor Relations Committee, and the Consultant's Advisory Committee for CUE. Phil has been called on multiple occasions to testify before Congress as an expert on union financial reporting and labor law reform.

About LRI Management Services, Inc.
LRI Management Services is a full-service labor relations consulting firm dedicated to the operational freedom, workplace tranquility and profitability of our clients It is a division of Labor Relations Institute, founded in 1978,

Order these publications
for <u>your</u> team today!

- ❑ *Comprehensive*—most labor topics covered
- ❑ *Thorough*—written by a labor lawyer
- ❑ *Handy*—designed to be <u>used</u>, not sit on a desk
- ❑ *Understandable*—no jargon, covers key concepts
- ❑ *Inexpensive*—beginning <u>**under $10**</u> each

CALL (800) 888-9115 or **Order Online** at
www.lrionline.com

YES! Send me the following tools for my team	Copies	Price	Total
Managing the Union Shop – 86-page guide for supervisors		$9.99 + shipping	
How to Investigate Grievances – 46-page guide for supervisors		$9.99 + shipping	
Model Contract Clauses – Over 200 model clauses (strong company and union proposals) plus drafting guide		$39.99+ shipping	
Reprimands for Union Shops –Nearly 100 sample letters of reprimand; document problems and win grievances		$29.99 + shipping	
Left of Boom: Putting Proactive Engagement to Work.		$39.99+ shipping	

Name	
Company Name	
Address	City/State/Zip
Phone	Email

Method of Payment ($20.00 minimum for credit card orders)

☐ Check (order shipped upon receipt) ☐ MasterCard
☐ Visa ☐ American Express

_____   _____

Card No. + 3-digit verification code (call if unsure of code)   Expiration Date

_____
Signature

www.ingramcontent.com/pod-product-compliance
Lightning Source LLC
Chambersburg PA
CBHW061142220326
41599CB00025B/4331